COUNTRY
ROADS OF
Louisiana

COUNTRY ROADS OF
Louisiana

by Glen Pitre
and Michelle Benoit

Country Roads Press
Oaks, Pennsylvania

Country Roads of Louisiana
© 1996 by Glen Pitre and Michelle Benoit. All rights reserved.

Published by Country Roads Press
P.O. Box 838, 2170 West Drive
Oaks, Pennsylvania 19456

Cover design by Caroline Hagen.
Cover illustration © 1996 by Michael McCurdy.
Illustrations by Victoria Sheridan.
Typesetting by Free Hand Press.

ISBN 1-56626-138-4
Library of Congress
Cataloging-in-Publication Data
    Country Roads of Louisiana / by Glen Pitre, Michelle Benoit
        p.   cm.
    Includes index
    ISBN 1-56626-138-4 (alk. paper)

    1. Louisiana-Guidebooks. 2. Automobile travel-Louisiana-
Guidebooks. I. Benoit, Michelle II. Title
F367.3.P58 1995
917.6304'63—dc20   95-9758
                                                          CIP

Printed in Canada.
10 9 8 7 6 5 4 3 2 1

To Margaret, queen of the road;

and Emelia and Loulan, who welcome us home again.

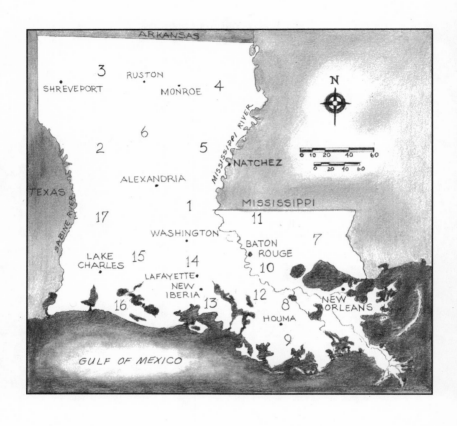

CONTENTS

ACKNOWLEDGMENTS

Thanks to everyone who made writing this book a rare treat; to Katheryn Krotzer-Laborde for her red pencil; to our staff for minding the store; to our families for lending beds, minding cats, and reminding us that, hey, most folks would kill to sightsee for a living. And to places we didn't visit — see you next time.

INTRODUCTION

There once was a farmer who had a pig. The farmer loved his pig, would do anything for it. The pig liked the farmer well enough, but what the pig really loved was persimmons.

One day a passing neighbor watched the farmer straining to hold up his pig so it could eat persimmons from a tree. Of course, the pig spent a great deal of time sniffing each persimmon first to be sure it was ripe before chomping into it.

"If you shook the tree, the ripe persimmons would fall," offered the neighbor, "Pig could eat 'em off the ground. Would save a lot of time."

The farmer considered the suggestion as he held high his beloved pig. "Sure," he finally shrugged. "But what's time to a pig?"

Like most people, we often think as the neighbor: get the job done, go from here to there in the shortest time possible. But this book is devoted to the hog-hugging farmer's point of view. Meandering the country roads of Louisiana, why not take the long way around when every turn leads to another scenic loop, when each fork holds adventurous possibilities? These tours are for leisurely travelers, poking around country lanes through areas the straight-line rush of interstate highways has forgotten.

If sometimes, like the farmer, our passions seem eccentric, our routes should nevertheless provide ample scenic, historic, culinary, and just plain odd-enough-to-be-fascinating points of interest and frequent opportunities to embark on digressions of your own. Pick and choose. Break chapters into bite-sized chunks to fit your schedule and travel plans.

Listen. The strings of a piney hills jamboree are calling. The rhythm of a Zydeco accordion urges toes to tap.

Sniff the air. What do you smell? Creole seafood gumbo? North Louisiana milk gravy, Cajun dirty rice, soul food mustard greens? Maybe Coushatta fried bread, Zwolle tamales, Natchitoches meat pies, Donaldsonville horseshoe loaves. Perhaps the subtler aromas of mayhaw jelly or old-fashioned strawberry wine.

Watch a Great Blue Heron two-thirds as tall as you are lumber into flight. Let yourself be dazzled by the roadside purple of iris and wisteria. The pink of azaleas and roseate spoonbills. The white of dogwoods and cotton fields. The blue of False River and Toledo Bend. The endless green of "trembling prairies" and pine vistas viewed from a hilltop.

Listen for ghosts. Homesick colonists and lovesick bandits. Singing governors and empires traded for a song. Fighting bishops, frolicking soldiers, conservationist Caroline Dormon and conversationalist Weeks Hall. And that's not to mention the still-breathing characters lurking behind every country store counter, roadside fence, checkered tablecloth, or state park uniform.

Louisiana is waiting, impatient to seduce you. So get in your car. Turn the key. Shift into drive.

And remember— *What's time to a pig?*

MB & GP, Lockport, LA 1995

For More Information:

Louisiana Office of Tourism 800-33-GUMBO
Louisiana Bed & Breakfast Association 504-346-1857
Kisatchie Nat'l Forest Recreation Directory 318-473-7160
Office of State Parks 504-342-8111

Museum and park entrance fees vary from free to about $4. Plantations run $5 to $10; swamp tours, $10 to $20. Occasional bridge and ferry tolls are minimal. Louisiana has no toll roads.

CHAPTER 1
HISTORY, HIKING, AND HOMEMADE PIE

ATON ROUGE to ALEXANDRIA via New Roads, Marksville, Lecompte, and Woodworth. One hundred and thirty-five miles past sugar cane and cotton plantations, Indian mounds, plant nurseries, nature areas, and antique shops.

"You look hungry!" was how the amiable clerk at Midway Grocery greeted us. Did it show that much? We'd only come a scant fifteen miles from Baton Rouge, exiting Interstate 10 at **Rosedale** to start our meandering journey north along Louisiana 77 and tree-shaded

Bayou Grosse Tete.

In a weathered 1903 mercantile building bedecked with old bottles and antique tools, the Midway is actually more deli than grocery store. At lunchtime, tables crowd with chatty locals.

"Sightseeing?" smiled the clerk as he stuffed a hunk of French bread for the po-boys we'd ordered to go. "Lots of plantations up the road."

The drive proved him right. Tree-shaded Louisiana 77 possesses lovely roadside views of mostly modest and closed-to-the-public country manors. An oak arbor nestles Trinity, an 1839 Louisiana colonial. Live Oak opens both its 1828 manor and mud-brick slave church to tours by appointment. Included is the tale of how its founder's father was killed by Andrew Jackson in a duel—yes, that Andrew Jackson—over a horse-race bet gone sour.

In southeast Louisiana, rivers didn't carve valleys like in most places; here they built land. Topsoil eroded from Nebraska, Ohio, and everywhere else upriver was deposited by floods onto the banks of streams to form broad frontlands, precious elevation in such soggy terrain. Settlers arriving too late for a seat at the main table, along the Mississippi River, would cross intervening swamp to where bayous like Grosse Tete (Gros Tate) provided narrower but equally fertile strips of relatively high land.

It's a geography Native Americans had understood long before. They, too, situated their villages and planted their corn and beans along the bayou bank. North of Rosedale, rambling Mound Plantation Home still sits perched high where it was built in 1840—atop an ancient Indian mound.

At **Maringouin**— in Cajun the name means "mosquito"—Louisiana 77 turns left through the sleepy railroad town. But we continued straight onto Louisiana 977, dodging chickens into a bayouside tunnel of green. One yard was cluttered with half-repaired tractors. Another was staked with orderly rows of knee-high sheet-metal tents, each with a bred-to-be-belligerent gamecock tethered just out of reach of his neighbors.

A mile past the square columns and rosy brick face of 1814 Valverda Plantation, the road rejoins Louisiana 77. A hop right is Joe's Restaurant in the 1920s Dreyfus Store. People drive here from considerable distances for fare a buddy describes as "like my grandmother's cooking—if grandmother was a cordon bleu chef."

Over the U.S. Route 190 bridge, go left through **Livonia** on Louisiana 78. Somewhere between Bayou Grosse Tete and False River, you'll make this tour's first of several crossings over the unmarked but very real boundary between English Louisiana and French Louisiana. Though time and television have blurred contrasts, you'll still see the distinction in the shapes of old houses and still hear the distinction in the shapes of vowels as your request for directions gets answered in an entirely different accent.

At False River, a right on Louisiana 1 leads to Louisiana 416, then Louisiana 415, the less-traveled long way round to New Roads past sugar-cane fields made famous in the novels of Ernest Gaines, who was reared at Riverlake Plantation. Caribbean-style mansions built by wealthy Haitian refugees (of the 1790s, not the 1990s) hide in the tangle of quiet woods. Overlooking False River, the Oxbow Restaurant boils crawfish from December to May and serves other tasty dishes year round. Anglers will enjoy Bonaventure's, a cafe that rents boats by the hour. And, of course, the whole route loops through the frontlands of where the Mississippi River used to be.

Huh? What was that—used to be?

When Louisiana's French founder Iberville passed here in 1699, False River was a bend of the Mississippi. But back then (before the Army Corps of Engineers), the great river frequently shifted course. One such switch cut off this twenty-three-mile-long curve, giving the parish its name, Pointe Coupée, and in effect making False River a lake. Fishermen, boaters, and water skiers have been grateful ever since.

Going left on Louisiana 1 leads to famous Parlange, an elegant 1750s Louisiana Colonial manor still inhabited by the family that built it. Take the tour, for Parlange's serene wide galleries, shaded by ancient oaks and flanked by brick *pigeonniers*, hide a surprisingly rich interior, almost as fanciful as the tales that accompany the house's colorful history.

Just past Parlange, the Pointe Coupée Museum & Tourist Center occupies a 1760 lakeside overseers cottage. We were enthralled by its two rooms of centuries-old homewares, including rare handwoven blankets. Even if you choose the long-way-round to New Roads, stop here first for driving-tour maps.

In **New Roads**, the Romanesque turrets and clock tower of the 1902 courthouse watch over antique shops, lunch spots, and a pleasant lake-front park. The side door of Gothic Revival St. Mary's Catholic Church is usually open. Inside, sunlight through German stained glass dapples St. Anthony's statue, where "found things" accumulate before the patron saint of "lost things." The click of our heels echoed as we walked to the painstakingly painted faux-marble pulpit and altar. We lit a candle to the church's talented artisans.

If you agree this area's charms deserve more than a day, many old lake-view houses offer bed and breakfast. Otherwise, from Louisiana 1 north, take Louisiana 10 east. Signs will announce the St. Francisville ferry ahead, but instead bear left onto Louisiana 420. Follow the high Mississippi River levee and a parade of plantations reflecting various cultures and eras— Creole, Greek Revival, Victorian—and the wood-frame St. Francis de Pointe Coupée Church, founded in 1728 as a mission to the Indians. Louisiana 420 rejoins Louisiana 1 near Morganza.

In 1927 the swollen Mississippi cratered its levees to flood 26,000 square miles. Hundreds drowned, and 637,000 were homeless. The Army Corps of Engineers was ordered to see that it didn't happen again. Past the village of **Morganza** is the huge Morganza Spillway. A modern-day engineer explains its purpose: "Know those overflow holes in your bathtub? Well, Morganza's one hundred and twenty five flood gates serve pretty much the same purpose, Except they're for when Mother Nature forgets to turn off the tap."

Louisiana 1 runs as straight as the nearby Union Pacific tracks, but the slower curves of River Road are enticing. At Batchelor's grain elevators, take Louisiana 419 right. Upriver, St. Stephen's Episcopal Church is venerable and well kept and proudly recalls more prosperous—and populous—days along the river. Its bricks and wooden pews were made on site by slaves in the 1850s, but the masters are the ones who are buried beneath the forest of stones and fragrant sweet olive behind the Gothic steeple. A Confederate soldier's cenotaph, "To Our Comrades," towers above them.

Beyond St. Stephen's, River Road is long and lonely even by our standards, so backtrack a quarter mile to Louisiana 971 and mosey beside tiny, overgrown Bayou Lettsworth. At Louisiana 1, turn right toward Marksville.

If traversing Morganza Spillway whetted your hunger for public works, from Louisiana 1 it's thirteen miles on Louisiana 15 to the gargantuan Old River Control Structure (tours by appointment). Forget mere flooding. This marvel keeps the Mississippi from changing course to pour down the Atchafalaya River, bypassing Baton Rouge and New Orleans entirely.

Across the Atchafalaya at **Simmesport**, a park commemorates the last battle of the Civil War's savage Red River Campaign. From there, road and railroad cut straight through the cotton and soybean fields of yet another floodway. Such a geographic tangle! The Red River, which starts in New Mexico, ends here. The Atchafalaya Basin, America's largest riverine swamp, starts here. And of course, North America's largest river keeps trying to jump its tracks near here. The resultant sloughs and bayous make a fecund habitat for hunting and fishing in nearby wildlife-management areas.

Louisiana 1 blares into **Marksville** past the throbbing eleven hundred slot machines and gaming tables of twenty-four-hour Grand Casino Avoyelles. (Its buffet, many locals claim, is the best restaurant in town.) Agreeing on a limit, we tried our luck. It took longer than we expected to lose our stake, but lose it we did.

Oh, well. Thankfully the riches of Marksville's Native American culture extend well beyond the reservation's casino. Just down the road, a pair of museums offers different but equally fascinating windows to the past.

Built to look like a ceremonial temple mound, the Tunica-Biloxi

Museum recounts the history of the small tribe that has lived here since the American Revolution. Among its collection is the tribe's prized and famous Tunica Treasure, a spectacular mix of native pottery and European trade wares from the 1700s. Examining the fat, luminescent blue and white trade beads, we understood why Stone Age Indians so esteemed them.

Off Louisiana 452, at the Marksville State Commemorative Area, we climbed the two-thousand-year-old earthen mounds that rise dramatically from the dense surrounding woods. An all-weather trail encircles extensive circular earthworks, ceremonial relics from a mysterious long-ago civilization that probably worshipped the sun. Inside the Mission-style interpretive center, excavated objects conjure images of this prehistoric people's daily life.

For a taste of French Creole life, visit nearby Mansura's Desfossé House or Marksville's Hypolite Bordelon House Museum on Louisiana 1 west of Main Street. The latter's fun mix of outbuildings includes a remarkable back-yard chapel built to shelter a grave. On the house itself, a bit of exposed wall reveals hand-hewn timbers and insulation made by mixing mud and Spanish moss into *bousillage*.

North on Main Street, downtown's landmarks include the red brick Queen Anne old Union bank and its replacement, the Beaux Arts new Union Bank. Each Easter, the 1927 Neoclassical courthouse hosts a tradition called egg knocking or egg *paquing* (*Pâques* means Easter). Gussied up in their holiday best, folks select decorated battle eggs by test-tapping them against their teeth. Old-timers guard secrets to strengthen eggshells. Others swear by guinea or goose eggs. Then the knocking begins, each egg against all comers! Hours later, the last egg left un-cracked is declared the champion.

Sauntering south, Main Street becomes Louisiana 115 for a dozen rural miles before joining Louisiana 29 at **Bunkie**, a railroad town named for a child's mispronounced pet monkey. Nowadays, it's a flea-market mecca; collectibles overflow old brick storefronts along U.S. Route 71. Behind downtown, the grand but silent Baily Hotel can only invoke nostalgia for Bunkie's glory days, but south and west, the

Parlange Plantation

grid of streets still hides fine old Creole and Victorian cottages.

After spending too much money antiquing, we headed northwest on U.S. Route 71 past the Epps House. In 1841, a moving chapter in African American history began when Solomon Northup, a free, educated black man, was kidnaped in New York, brought south, and auctioned into slavery. His bondage on the Epps place forms part of his famous chronicle, *Twelve Years a Slave.*

Bayou Boeuf (Beff) marks re-entry into plantation country. On the left, an oak alley graces Buebenzer (private). The bayou meanders away to the right with signs for Walnut Grove. (Ignore them; a prettier route to it lies ahead.) Quaint Gothic arches shield the weathered porch of the 1854 Bennett Plantation Store. Across the road sits its equally timeworn "big house."

Eli Whitney perfected a gin to remove seeds from cotton bolls in 1793, shortly after the steamboat's arrival. The two inventions made cotton king along the rivers of the South, including Bayou Boeuf. Early French settlers here were overwhelmed by an 1811 influx of South Carolina Protestants looking for good cotton land. They found it.

Mid-September to mid-November, along roadside fields, tractor-trailer-sized modules of harvested cotton wear colorful rain bonnets as they await trucking to Cheneyville's Producers Mutual Cotton Gin. "We yield 20,000 bales in a decent year," avows Thelma McCann, who conducts the free tour through the gin (call ahead). Big, roaring machines suck up field-dirty lint and out fluffs pristine white cotton. Fuzzy black seeds dance out of a chute underneath.

"Nothing goes to waste. Seeds are pressed for oil. The residue's made into chicken feed. Leaves and trash rot into what we call black dirt. Good compost for gardens," Ms. McCann touts. "And free to anybody who'll haul it away. Want some?"

In **Cheneyville**, a right at the light onto Klock Street leads through town and back to the bayou. Across it, turn right for Federal-style Walnut Grove with its relic formal gardens that were once every plantation's pride. Or turn left to Trinity Episcopal Church, consecrated by Leonidas Polk in 1861, just before he strapped on his sword to become the Confederacy's Fighting Bishop. Follow Bayou Boeuf amid cotton fields shoulder to shoulder with sugar cane back to U.S. Route 71 north. At U.S. Route 167, follow the signs to Loyd Hall Plantation.

This magnificent manor with combination Italianate and Greek Revival façade, broad upper-floor galleries, and high-ceilinged rooms elaborate with plasterwork was being used as a hay barn when the current owner's parents discovered it in 1948. Maybe that's why this working plantation manages so comfortably to fuse gorgeous antiques with relaxed country living. Now fully restored, Loyd Hall offers both tours and a bed and breakfast.

The old Civil War "military road" (Louisiana 456), parallel to and just west of U.S. Route 71, snakes north past the colossal brick ruins of Meeker Sugar Mill. A fellow we met swore Meeker once "cooked all the molasses that used to coat Cracker Jacks."

Ahead lies a crackerjack treat of another sort. Lea's Lunchroom, at Louisiana 112 and U.S. Route 71, is a long-time statewide breakfast, lunch, and dinner favorite. The cured ham is famous. The pies... Oh! The pies! Even after gorging past the point of good manners, we bought a couple for the road. Well, pies *can* last a while in a cooler if you keep them out of the ice water…and your mouth.

Lecompte (Luh-COUNT) was named for a local thoroughbred, Lecomte, who won fame in the Great New Orleans Stakes Race of 1854. The "p" was added by a careless railroad sign painter. From the old Wall Street hardware store, weave north through the village to the Old Lecompte High School Museum where exhibits chronicle Bayou Boeuf history. We especially enjoyed 1890s photos of free-wheeling Wall Street saloons and the farming artifacts upstairs. With three stories of classrooms, there's plenty of display space. A volunteer guide confided, "We're trying to get Lecomte's tail."

Lecompte's tale?

"No, Lecomte's tail—the racehorse. Seems his tail's been sitting in a Baton Rouge bank vault for the last hundred and forty years or so, and we're trying to get it for the museum."

Maybe the tail will be hanging there when you visit. Either way, head north on Hardy Street toward "sugar loop," the scenic route out of town. Just before Lamourie Bayou bridge, turn left to St. John the Baptist, a rare, surviving gingerbreaded Civil War-era African American church. Across the bridge, go left on Louisiana 470 and left again onto Chickamaw Road, a sinewy country trail of family farms and cypress-swamp bayou that exits back onto Louisiana 112.

Westward Louisiana 112 crosses Bayou Boeuf, out of bottomland and into piney hills. Traversing Interstate 49, a few plant nurseries spring up. Then more nurseries. And more! If it seems there are hundreds of them, it's because there are. Since 1900, when "Grandpa" Samuel Stokes started selling holly and jasmine that he'd dug up in the woods, the wholesale nursery business has become Forest Hill's claim to fame. Tempted to stop? Watch for occasional "We Sell Retail" signs.

Two miles north on pine-lined U.S. Route 165, a historical marker notes the sparse ruins of Camp Claiborne where half a million young Americans trained for World War II. A few foundations remain as monuments to the young men who were gathered from tenement and farm, each excited at seeing the world, yet each apprehensive at being asked to save it.

At the village of **Woodworth,** named for a long-ago sawmill executive perhaps as compensation for a career's worth of bad puns about his name, the Woodworth Corner Store masquerades as an oversized gas-station—convenience mart. Inside is camping gear and hiking info. No better spot for it, because east from this crossroads, Louisiana 22 leads to Indian Creek Recreation Area and, beyond it, Alexander State Forest. The latter's headquarters in a 1935 Civilian Conservation Corps log cabin is a worthwhile visit in itself.

To the west lies the fabled Wild Azalea Trail. Entering the forest a mile past Woodworth Town Hall, this thirty-one-mile-long (but easy) federal hiking trail blooms delicate pink azaleas and white dogwood from mid-March to mid-April. Alternate access points, numerous shorter trails (including an especially beautiful one along Kincaid Reservoir), and intersections with gravel Forest Service Roads beget inexhaustible possibilities. Camping fifty feet off trail is allowed.

As it approaches Alexandria, U.S. Route 165 sprouts a median, frontage roads, and motels, so let's end the chapter in these woods, atune to the night sounds. Come a little closer, Hon. Let me put my arm around you as we listen to the crickets and let our eyes adjust to the twilight.

For more information:

Iberville Parish Tourist Commission 800-233-3560
    P.O. Box 248, Plaquemine, LA 70765
Live Oak Plantation 504-648-2346
    P.O. Box 202, Rosedale, LA 70772
Pointe Coupée Tourist Commission 504-638-3500
    P.O. Box 555, New Roads, LA 70760

Parlange Plantation 504-638-8410
    New Roads, LA 70760
Old River Control Structure 504-492-2169
    AHC-63 Box 205-A, Vidalia, LA 71373
Avoyelles Parish Tourist Commission 318-253-9208
    301 North Main, Marksville, LA 71351
Marksville State Commemorative Area 318-253-8954
    700 Martin Luther King Drive, Marksville, LA 71351
Producer's Mutual Cotton Gin 318-279-2145
    P.O. Box 278, Cheneyville, LA 71325
Loyd Hall Plantation and Bed and Breakfast 318-776-5641
    292 Loyd Bridge Road, Cheneyville, LA 71325
Wild Azalea Trail Info via Kisatchie Forest 318-445-9396
    3727 Government Street, Alexandria, LA 71302
Rapides Parish/Alexandria Visitors Bureau 318-443-7049
    P.O. Box 8110, Alexandria, LA 71306

CHAPTER 2

THE RED RIVER VALLEY

From **ALEXANDRIA to SHREVEPORT**, via Bayou Rapides, Cane River, Natchitoches, and Mansfield, about a hundred and sixty miles, not counting a couple of optional spurs. Features antebellum homes, colonial sites, hiking trails, pecan orchards, battlefields, and a hidden chapel.

Alexandria (usually shortened to ELL-ick) began in 1723 as the settlement Les Rapides. During low-water on the Red River, boats had to be off-loaded to get over limestone shoals here, then reloaded upstream. As Glen strained to pack our Plymouth with enough supplies to equip a small army, he failed to appreciate the irony.

Leave Alex via Louisiana 496 (Bayou Rapides Road) by starting at Kent House. One of the few lower Red River plantations to survive the Civil War, this fine colonial home's period furniture, herb and formal gardens, quarters, milk house, and other features paint a vivid picture of 1800s plantation life.

Scarcely a mile west, fields of cotton alternate with *allées* of cedars or groves of oaks that mark gracious Bayou Rapides plantations and bygone hamlets. The road traces the bayou's bends, its waters laconic then suddenly dancing in a sparkle across small shoals. Across the bayou, **McNutt** is dominated by its cotton gin and the now-closed Blue Star Store, a great example of an old-time plantation commissary. From McNutt, continue north on Louisiana 121 with Bayou Rapides on the left.

A couple of miles farther, slow for a glimpse of Juliette (private), a late-1860s rebuilt-on-Civil-War-ashes plantation home half hidden on the left. It's as far again to **Hot Wells**, where Louisiana 1200 leads a mile south to Cotile Lake Recreation Area, a relaxing picnic and fishing spot; and Louisiana 1201 enters Hot Wells proper, site of a closed mineral-water spa.

When Louisiana 121 ends, turn left onto Louisiana 1. The road finds an alley northwest between Interstate 49 and the swamps that hug the Red River, then climbs gentle rolls of pine forest. A bridge crosses Cane River where once did Monnett's Ferry. In April 1864, near the end of the Red River Campaign, three hundred Union troops were killed or wounded trying to wade this spot, fleeing their defeat at Mansfield and burning every plantation along the way.

But Cane River had an even more consequential contribution to the Civil War's beginning. Near the town of Chopin stood a plantation estate that legend says inspired *Uncle Tom's Cabin: Life Among the Lowly*. That 1852 best-selling novel, by personalizing the ordeals of slavery, hastened the war that would end it. Once a tourist attraction known as Little Eva Plantation, today neither big house nor slave cabins remain. But every October and November, visitors stop for

Little Eva's pecan harvest.

Where endless stretches of pecan trees canopy miles of close cropped grass, the Red Barn adds folk art and food products to its offering of pecans. Across the road, Natchitoches Pecans hails your sweet tooth with locally made candies. Both sell nuts by the pound or by the sack, whole, cracked, or shelled. Glimpses of Cane River tease across cotton fields.

At Louisiana 491, turn right into **Cloutierville** (CLOO-chur-vill). Over the bridge and past the old Murray Cotton Gin, two monumental magnolias frame Bayou Folk Museum. Profuse and eclectic artifacts, from nineteenth-century wedding dresses to ornate coffins, from a fully equipped doctor's office to a likewise outfitted blacksmith shop, fill this elaborately furnished home of Cloutierville's founder and, later, of author Kate Chopin.

Cloutierville's lovely and unpretentious Creole architecture marks the southern tip of an island of Gallicism in largely Anglo-Saxon Protestant north Louisiana. As one lifelong resident told us, "We spoke French, ate Spanish, and went to Catholic Church."

It's a mile and a half up Louisiana 1 to Louisiana 119's crossroads and Derry Mercantile. Though its menu is scant, this empty-shelved plantation store feeds lunch to a small but loyal clientele. How many places grind fresh beef every time someone orders a burger?

A left on Louisiana 119 detours to Kisatchie National Forest's Longleaf Trail. This scenic byway weaves seventeen miles through towering pines and unique wolds, so prepare for short hikes. Maps at the unmanned kiosk on the way in outline paths to dramatic bluffs, rocky rapids, and overlooks of the pine and hardwood forests. The trail ends at Louisiana 117 to rejoin this chapter's route on Louisiana 6 between Natchitoches and Robeline.

A right on Louisiana 119 heads from Louisiana 1 across a bridge toward another beautiful drive with the Cane River weaving into view on the left and cotton fields blending into oak-umbrellaed farmsteads on the right. Magnolia Plantation, a working farm in the same family since 1753, offers tours of the 1868 big house. Its adjacent

1830s cotton press and chapel are scheduled to become a National Park Service attraction.

In antebellum Louisiana, not all African Americans were slaves. Some *gens de couleur libres* were artisans, mechanics, and ironworkers. Other free people of color were planters, and especially along Cane River, many owned slaves themselves.

At Melrose Plantation, cattle graze under orderly ranks of pecan trees receding into the distance. Founded before the Louisiana Purchase by former slave Marie Thérèse Coincoin, Melrose's is a tale worthy of the fascinating house and outbuildings, as well as the artistic riches of its later guests and most famous occupant.

When we reached its gates, a tame blue jay literally led us up the brick path winding its way under mammoth oaks. When we entered the house, it flew in. When we paused to explain our mission to the tour guide, the impatient jay lifted the edge of a hand-out. Transfixed by the bird's cleverness, we missed much of what the guide told us, but we'd visited here before. For Louisiana book lovers, Melrose is a shrine.

Through much of the early twentieth century, plantation mistress Cammie Henry invited writers to work here. National figures like John Steinbeck and Heywood Broun, Louisiana's own Lyle Saxon and Caroline Dormon, and many others came. Clementine Hunter, America's best-known primitive artist after Grandma Moses, had been a cook at Melrose and continued to paint here until her death in 1988 at age 101; an upstairs *garçonnière* is now a gallery of her work. Five outbuildings are on the tour, including America's best surviving example of African-influenced architecture.

At Melrose, Louisiana 493 crosses the river to **Isle Brevelle**, a Creole community. To the left of the bridge is St. Augustine Church, with a beautiful view of the Cane River and a cemetery telling of local history. Inside is a proud portrait of Augustin Metoyer, Melrose owner and church founder.

The LaCour Doll House is a skip ahead, right on Louisiana 1. Inside, a two-year-old child slept curled on one of the quilts which, together with hand-sewn dolls, crowd the one-room store. "Been sewing since I was a little girl," Mrs. LaCour told us as she stitched a pillow. "If you needed a quilt, you made it. Wanted a doll, you made it." Today, she makes them for collectors throughout the South.

Back on Cane River, Louisiana 119 continues north through more pecan groves, cotton fields, and pastures of prancing thoroughbreds. Bear right on Louisiana 494 for Cane River's parade of plantations: Oakland, Beau Fort, Cherokee, Oaklawn. Only Beau Fort, famous for its eighty-four-foot-long front gallery, offers tours.

Over the bridge into **Natchitoches**, the first cross street is Louisiana 6. To your left waits Fort St. Jean Baptiste; to your right are thirty three blocks of the oldest town in the Louisiana Purchase. Natchitoches has a long list of bed and breakfasts and no shortage of things to do, from sampling famed meat pies to strolling quaint shops or partaking of a riverboat cruise. Popular seasons to visit are during the October Pilgrimage, when many town homes and plantations open their doors, and during the Christmas Festival of Lights. At the north end of old downtown, a bust of city founder, Louis Juchereau de St. Denis, oversees the well-stocked visitors center. Be sure to ask for a map as this old settlement's street layout is sometimes eccentric.

Now back to Fort St. Jean. This history buff's dream replicates one of the log stockades begun in 1714 by St. Denis as a stronghold against—and illegal trading post with—Spanish Texas. St. Denis was a real-life swashbuckler who explored the wilderness, who was adopted by the Caddo and fought the Natchez, who was imprisoned in Mexico but won release by romancing the commandant's granddaughter, who... O.K., O.K. We'll let the fort's well-versed park rangers bring to life that pivotal fellow's time.

Briarwood is a thirty-mile side trip that nature lovers must take. Follow Louisiana 6/U.S. Route 84 north out of Natchitoches. Admire the west-bank bluffs of Grand Ecore, historically Natchitoches' port, as you cross Red River. As marshaling site for the Civil War Union retreat, Grand Ecore marked the northern end of what was known for decades afterwards as "the burnt district."

At Clarence, turn left on U.S. Route 71, then, just past Campti, go right on Louisiana 9 north over cypress-ringed Black Lake. Its north shore offers lodges, restaurants, and boat rentals for superb lake fishing.

From there, it's about 15 miles to Briarwood. This corner of Kisatchie National Forest, open every weekend in April, May, August, and November, is a spellbinding spot with trails through huge old-growth longleaf pines, azaleas, iris bogs, and dogwood clusters. What makes it even more special is the very remarkable woman who called it home.

Caroline Dormon was an environmentalist long before most Americans ever heard the word. When she wasn't ferreting out species of Louisiana iris, she was saving dwindling longleaf pines. When politicians turned a deaf ear, she simply lobbied their wives. Her efforts won Louisiana the first National Forest east of the Rockies and won her employment as the first woman in the U.S. Forest Service. At Briarwood, Miss Carrie spent her final years nurturing native plants. Her log cabin, now a museum, and her writing cottage are tucked into the woods she loved.

As long as you've come this far, go another half mile north to the old-fashioned, one-block town of **Saline** (Suh-LEEN). While there, we tramped its covered sidewalk to investigate a rhythmic plap, plap, plap coming from behind a dusty picture window painted "Law Office and Notary." The sound came not from an attorney's document-spitting fax machine but instead from a table of elderly gents slapping dominoes in spirited contest.

Back in Natchitoches, on Louisiana 6 west is Los Adaes (uh-DYE-us), site of a Spanish mission declared the capital of Texas in 1729. A mile farther, we entered **Robeline** (ROW-ba-leen) for a right turn at Louisiana 120. After woods and farms and the village of **Marthaville**, turn right again onto Louisiana 1221, past ponds and chicken farms to Rebel Commemorative Area.

If you're starting to feel lost, you're not the first. During the Civil War, a lost Confederate soldier stopped here at the Barnhill farm for a drink of water. When he was shot by Union troops a short while later, the farmer buried him. Succeeding generations of Barnhills tended the stranger's grave until the state assumed the obligation a century later.

Let's hope the nameless soldier was a music lover, because Rebel Commemorative Area has evolved into an institution that has nothing to do with warfare. A spiffy museum shaped like a musical note pays homage to traditional piney-woods music. Displays and recordings explain gospel, old-time, rockabilly, and more. Out back among the pines, a natural amphitheater seats a thousand for evening concerts and the Louisiana Fiddling Championship in April.

Humming "Shall We Gather by the River," we backtracked to Louisiana 120 west, continuing along the Union Army's path during the Red River Campaign. At the crossroads hamlet of Belmont, turn north onto Louisiana 175. Just past the junction with Louisiana 177 in **Pleasant Hill** is the site of Old Pleasant Hill and a collection of historical markers of the biggest Civil War battle west of the Mississippi.

Unlike the usual terse bronze plaques dotting the roadside, these grand slabs of polished marble are engraved with entire 1864 newspaper articles, generals' battlefield reports, an ode to dead soldiers. Most intense is a "You are there" account on the farthest marker. Read it aloud for a visceral sickening thrill, a shadow of the horror that happened at this very spot.

Just up Louisiana 175 stands the last remaining Civil War-vintage house in Pleasant Hill, a dogtrot pioneer cabin. Across the road was an American Legion Hall with a drive-thru window. Curious, we drove through. "Do you have any historical brochures?" we asked.

A yellow-haired woman leaned out. "We got package liquor. Bourbon, Scotch...." Spying a wall of bottles behind her, we could see she was serious; and she saw how surprised we were.

"How about a soft drink?" she asked, changing her tactics.

We ordered a soda and sounded retreat, not quite sure where an American Legion Civil War battlefield drive-thru liquor store fit into the grand scheme of the cosmos.

Plaques marking advances and withdrawals stud the next fifteen miles to the split-rail fence of the Battle of Mansfield Commemorative Area. An excellent interpretive center explains this last major Confederate victory of the Civil War. Though the next day's fight at Pleasant Hill was bloodier, it was basically a draw, the proverbial "sound and fury, signifying nothing." At **Mansfield**, thirty-six thousand Union troops backed by a fleet of eighty Red River gunboats abandoned plans to invade Texas and, not incidentally, confiscate cotton to feed idled New England textile mills.

Mansfield itself is a typical north Louisiana courthouse town—founded on cotton, built on railroads, boomed on oil, and hanging on with wood products for the last half century. But Michelle remembered a spot nearby where her mother once took her, a place called the little Rock Chapel.

From Louisiana 175, take Louisiana 509 six miles northeast, turning right at the sign for Carmel Baptist Church. At Laffitte Store, leave a donation and pick up the keys that, a half mile farther, open the gate to a secluded hilltop arbor. Beyond a giddy brook, a row of graves leads to a small vault of coarse stone, the remains of an 1850s wilderness monastery. Inside, colorful wall and ceiling frescoes of fierce griffins and a fabulous phoenix reminded us of hilltop chapels we'd seen in Croatia. For a moment, we forgot we were in the modern Bible Belt and could almost hear the chant of these long-dead European monks.

Back through Mansfield, north on U.S. Route 71 is **Grand Cane**. At the center of the single ghost-town block, the local bank's gracefully arched storefront is long closed but in pristine condition. We pressed our faces to the glass, peering at the mahogany counters and wood-screen teller's window. Who were the immigrant merchants that saved their hard-won dimes here? Who were the proud farmers that came hat in hand to extend a crop loan?

We continued north. Where U.S. Route 71 becomes four lanes for the final twenty miles to Shreveport, we decided yet to prolong our trip with a detour on Louisiana 5 west to **Keatchie** (Keetch-EYE).

Fresh-painted chapels welcomed us to a village where most of the remarkable wood frame buildings are on the National Register. Between the Masonic lodge and a huge store, Louisiana 172 leads to another storybook church and what remains of a women's college that doubled as Confederate hospital after the battle of Mansfield.

Leaning against our trusty Plymouth, we listened as the breeze through weathered clapboards became the giggles of the college girls who studied here more than a hundred years ago.

For more information:

Kent House 318-487-5998
    3601 Bayou Rapides Road, Alexandria, LA 71303
Bayou Folk Museum/Kate Chopin House 318-379-2233
    Cloutierville, LA 71416
Kisatchie Longleaf Trail Scenic Byway 318-352-2568
    Highway 6 West, Natchitoches, LA 71457
Magnolia Plantation 318-379-2221
    5487 Highway 119, Natchez, LA 71456
Melrose Plantation 318-352-4411
    Box 2248, Natchitoches, LA 71457
Beau Fort Plantation 318-352-9580
    4055 Highway 494, Natchitoches, LA 71457
Natchitoches Tourist Bureau 800-259-1714
    P.O. Box 411, Natchitoches, LA 71458
Briarwood - Caroline Dormon Nature Preserve 318-576-3379
    P.O. Box 226, Natchitoches, LA 71457
Fort St. Jean-Baptiste 318-357-3101
    103 Morrow, Natchitoches, LA 71458
Rebel Commemorative Area 318-472-6255
    P.O. Box 127, Marthaville, LA 71456
Mansfield Commemorative Area 318-872-1474
    Route 2, Box 459, Mansfield, LA 71052
DeSoto Chamber of Commerce/Rock Chapel 318-872-1310
    210 South Washington, Mansfield, LA 71052 ....

CHAPTER 3
BLUES, OIL, AND MILK GRAVY

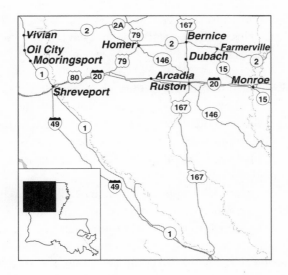

 rom **SHREVEPORT to MONROE**, zigzagging between U.S. Route 80 and the Arkansas line. Two hundred and twenty-five circuitous miles of piney hills, lakes, country cooking, dogtrot houses, and Bonnie and Clyde.

Shreveport to Monroe is a ninety-six-mile straight shot on Interstate 20, so to say we're taking you the long way 'round may win some prize for understatement. But from our route, possible short cuts abound, and you'll often be only minutes from the interstate. So let's start our journey east... by going west.

Interstate 20 west's early-morning traffic flung us out of Shreveport and onto Louisiana 169 where we slowed to a northward stroll. Amidst dense woods, one of the scattered homesteads proffered "Homemade Quilts," but we decided that even in the country, the morning was a bit too young to go knocking on someone's door.

At the hamlet of **Longwood** (Louisiana 169's intersection with Blanchard-Furrh Road), the Stumpwater Inn promises hot lunches, memorable homemade pies, and fascinating old farm relics—but not breakfast. The Longwood General Store across the way is a local mull-over-your-coffee spot decorated with a relaxed assortment of old signs and artifacts. Three miles east, the Jacobs Nature Park offers hiking through scenic woods.

Continue north to **Mooringsport** where tiny downtown tempts with the Doll Shop and Hospital, a stately Masonic Lodge and Kennedy's Country Store. Mosey between the steamboat-busy "1837 Mooring's Port" mural and the local minimuseum to admire the eerie drama of Caddo Lake. Or visit Belle of the Bluff cafe and junk shop by the railroad tracks.

The woods near Mooringsport are where Leadbelly was born. The folk-blues legend honed his vocal talents shouting morning hellos to neighbors near enough to hear him but too distant to see. We tried a little call and response across our bucket seats, but settled for crooning his classics "Goodnight, Irene" and "Midnight Special."

North across Caddo Lake, Louisiana 538 tops a narrow isthmus. Oil wells sticking out of the water, bobbing there since 1911, mark the world's first offshore drilling. The oil they pump might be fueling your road hog right now; maybe they fueled your great-grandparents' Model T as well.

Oil City on Louisiana 1 was the site of north Louisiana's first gusher. You won't doubt it after seeing lawns, mailboxes, and belt buckles decorated with replica oil derricks. A local deli calls itself "Gusher Mart." In prominent-citizen Dub Allen's front yard, a unique, jet-age welcome sign announces, "Oil City, A City on the Ball." A left at the quaint frame sheriff's office just past the welcome ball borders a de-lightful lakeside park. Picnic tables overlook a playground and fish-ing piers reach into the cypress-studded lake.

Savage Street, a block before the town's only light, heads east to Land Avenue and the Caddo-Pine Island Oil Museum. Even if closed, its outdoor display of oil-field machinery and the wood-frame Trees Oil Company building across the street are memorable. Downtown Oil City is a pristine block bookended with bright murals and dotted with "Dub Allen" park benches.

The pace of change here can best be measured by the fact that "Ro-tary Meets Wednesday" is inscribed in neon over the door of the Oil City Restaurant and Big Man's Barbecue. Yet, Oil City has changed from its 1910s boomtown days when men and oxen crowded these streets on their way to the wells, passing a tree in the middle of Main Street used to chain up drunks and other offenders from the overcrowded jail.

Inside the Oil City Restaurant, behind dining rooms adorned with photos of Dub Allen's political rise, was a kitchen alive with activity. Owner and chef Mary Graham, dressed for church under her white apron, emptied a vat of chopped mustard greens into a steaming cauldron of sauteed onions. "Where'd you learn to cook like this?" we asked, heady on the aroma. Mary laughed as she cut up a strip of salt pork, her brown fingers a blur. "Growing up just south of here, in a town too small to make the map. There were only three houses: our house, the outhouse, and the hen house."

Louisiana 1 continues north to **Vivian** with its "21 churches to meet your spiritual needs" and where Bauer Hardware Store offers bridal registry. At the Stagecoach Junction Antique Mall and Mu-seum, take a left onto Louisiana Avenue. A half block down, Re-Creations Musicke Shoppe crafts dulcimers, zithers, and the like, welcoming visitors to "play, sing, or just listen." The corner drugstore boasts an old-time soda fountain. Spinning around on swivel stools and snitching tastes of each other's phosphates, we realized we were falling in love with this corner of Louisiana.

Doubling back east, Louisiana Avenue dead-ends at the old depot, now the Louisiana Redbud Museum. The what museum? Hey, just drop south a block to Louisiana 2 and turn left, east out of town. Weaving through neighborhoods filled with redbuds during February and March, you'll declare these vivid pink trees deserve the festival and museum Vivian gives them. As visually hypnotic as the redbuds, outside town there are three miles of pumping oil wells that go up and down, up and down.... Here, deep below the orange-colored earth, is the reason Vivian boomed during the 1909 oil rush.

Hardwoods mix with pines along the lonely roadside. Cypress rise from the water at Black Bayou Lake. After jogging left at Hosston, Louisiana 2 leaves the woods for flat bottom-land cotton fields. Crossing the Red River, piney hills take over once more. Redbud trees adorn the yards of the occasional home place.

Through Plain Dealing, then Sarepta. At Shongaloo, Louisiana 2 splits. Take Louisiana 2 Alternate, past a fine 1909 white farmhouse. From there, the woods are infrequently broken by a farm or B.C. (local shorthand for Baptist Church) until **Haynesville**, home of the September Claiborne Parish Fair, where a handful of fine houses from the town's 1921 oil boom grace U.S. Route 79 north of downtown. Perhaps Haynesville's greatest fame comes from being birthplace of designer Geoffrey Beene (given name, Samuel Bozeman).

For us, the attraction was more personal. Michelle's mother, Margaret, was accompanying us, and Haynesville is where she spent her grade-school years. Near the village center, we found the passenger depot, now a feed store, where Mom and her classmates sang for Al Smith when he whistle-stopped through while running for president against Herbert Hoover.

Follow U.S. Route 79 south to **Homer**, where the Linder Lodge Restaurant pits its enormous buffet lunch against the one served at the Sunrise Bakery and Restaurant downtown. Massive white columns of the pre-Civil War courthouse dominate a compact, thriving business district. Among its banks and clothing stores sits one of the state's most phenomenal museums.

Dogtrot House

Filling the 1890 Victorian Italianate Hotel Claiborne, the Ford Museum hosts an incredibly diverse collection of artifacts and displays. In room after room, everything from Native American pottery cooking balls to ingenious nineteenth-century farming equipment to spinning wheels, looms, and homespun clothing to an authentic log cabin are arranged with panache and a sense of history to tell the story of the North Louisiana hill country.

The docents at the Ford can also guide you to several appealing detours that start from Homer: The Arizona community nestled on the eastern edge of lovely Lake Claiborne has a museum and several old sites; the Alberry Wasson House northeast near Summerfield is the only two-story log dogtrot left in the state. (What's a dogtrot? Keep reading.)

Something more outdoorsy? Take Louisiana 146 ten miles southeast to Lake Claiborne State Park. Wooded hills drop right into the big blue lake. Fishing is great, water skiing popular, and there's a beach for swimming. Nearby private facilities supplement the park's public boat rentals and campsites.

In the 1830s, German idealists voyaged thousands of miles to the piney-hills wilderness south of Homer to create a utopia. The Germantown Colony where Countess von Leon and her followers lived for thirty seven years is off U.S. Route 79 south. A right on Parish Road 111, then again on Parish Road 114 leads to the replicated buildings surrounding three original dwellings, including the countess's own. Though she had her house decorated with fancy wallpaper and filled with the music of her piano, the frontier hardship which the museum brings to life must have seemed to her so very far from civilized old Europe.

Caney Lake Recreation Area, off Parish Road 111, is part of Kisatchie National Forest. Its Sugar Cane Trail snakes over seven miles through forests, over hills, past lake views and even the ruins of an old mill where locals had their ribbon cane rendered to syrup.

South on U.S. Route 79 is the charming downtown of **Minden**. Four blocks of brick streets harbor Pace's Sanitary Barber Shop, a great original neon at the Western Auto, a Knights of Pythias Lodge, a used book store, and a terrific coin shop. At the sidewalk clock, feast on the green-glazed facade of the Bank of Minden. A block south, running the other direction, residential Broadway is lined with fine old houses. Union Street (U.S. Route 80 east) leaves Minden for a leisurely drive to Arcadia, past old farm houses and the occasional wood-products mill.

If your tastes run to cops and robbers, take a side trip to Bonnie and Clyde's ambush site. At Gibbsland, turn off U.S. Route 80 onto Louisiana 154, through the Tater Hill yam farm to Mt. Lebanon. Just before the Stagecoach Trail Museum, follow Louisiana 154's hard right. Across the road from the stately old Mt. Lebanon Baptist Church, the big white house on a hill is actually a fancied-up dogtrot. (We'll explain, promise.) Five miles farther, past old red barns, the road climbs the hill that Sheriff Jordan and his posse had been tipped off was the "mail box" where the murderous bank robbers picked up messages from their accomplices. Today, the site's stone marker is pitted by amateur target shooters, a fitting reminder perhaps to what happened here in May of 1934.

Returning to Gibbsland, it's seven miles to **Arcadia**. Entering on U.S. Route 80, Sharon's Cafe offers hot-water bread, greens, grits, yams, and the like in heaping, mouth-watering lunch specials. Breakfast is no less satiating: great pancakes, biscuits, and milk gravy. The latter was a new experience for south Louisiana-born Glen who eyed it with skepticism, but after a taste, then a slurp, milk gravy had won another convert.

At Arcadia's center, the railroad depot waits transformation into a museum. Old downtown is not nearly so spiffy as Homer or Minden, but strolling the sprawl of raised, covered sidewalks, we found charm in the fact that the classic old bank building still houses a bank, and that not just tourists but also local residents shop the arcade, passing through old glass doors to fill a prescription, get a hair cut, or buy an ad in the weekly *Bienville Democrat*.

Of course, our impressions were influenced by Michelle's very excited mother, for this was another place she'd lived as her dentist father chased the north Louisiana oil rush from town to town. Margaret's old high school burned long ago, but concrete bleachers yet overlook its football field. Here she gave the Arcadia High valedictory address. But strange how the human mind works, for what she flashed back to was not that graduation speech, but a football cheer: "Peas, beans, okra, squash! Can they beat us? No, by gosh!" And how upset her mom was to hear a near-swear-word like "gosh."

Margaret led us down the alley behind the First National Bank where she and a few hundred others queued for a peek at the cleaned-up but bullet-ridden corpses of Bonnie and Clyde, laid out at a makeshift morgue in back of a furniture store. Nowadays, Arcadia remembers that gory incident with Bonnie & Clyde Trade Days. Motel rooms fill fast the weekend before the third Monday of every month as over a thousand flea-market booths hawk their wares to treasure hunters from near and far. Other times, an outlet mall on Interstate 20 serves as a bargain hunter's consolation prize.

East of Arcadia, U.S. Route 80 rolls over cow-dotted hills beside the Illinois Central Gulf tracks through **Simsboro** and **Grambling**. The decades-long reign of famed coach Eddie Robinson won Grambling State University the nickname "Cradle of the Pros," making it one of America's best-known predominantly African American universities. Just inside **Ruston** city limits, Louisiana Tech Farm Sales Room offers a cornucopia of milk, ice cream, meat, vegetables, cheese, and potted plants, all produced on the university's experimental farm. We loaded up our cooler, obeying a fellow customer who promised, "Once you taste what these college cows do, you'll never buy store-bought milk again."

U.S. Route 80 turns into California Street, a collegiate frenzy of fast food and strip malls. Take a left on U.S. Route 167 north to the cluster of tempting downtown shops.

In an old movie house, the Dixie Jamboree twangs with Saturday evening piney hills music shows. The Jamboree is but one of the charms making Ruston a good overnight destination. Even if you can't stay over, make sure there's time to eat at Sarah's. Not only is the vegetarian soul food delicious, but the restaurant itself is a mystical experience, with Bible quotes painted onto the front walk and a trip through the kitchen necessary to reach your table. At 607 Lee Avenue it's a little tricky to get to, but as Sarah herself will tell you, so is the Promised Land.

North of town on U.S. Route 167, fall brings reds and yellows to the hardwoods mixed in with the rolling pines. In **Dubach**, the grand, columned 1901 home of timberman founder Fred Dubach is the town's pride, but Hamilton and Sons downtown, which still sells bolts of cloth and hardware beside its canned goods and groceries, is its heart. Dubach also lays claim to being "Dogtrot Capital," so here you get to visit one.

A mile west of town on Hico Street, the 1849 log Autrey House is the oldest structure hereabouts. Three rooms wide under a single roof line, in classic dogtrot style, the center room has no walls front nor rear. It's like a porch except it runs through the middle of the house, open to the breeze. A plaque recounts the journey of Absaz lom Autrey

from an Alabama hill farm to the grave out back where he's flanked
by the two wives he outlived. The origins of the dogtrot style are
considerably more obscure. Once popular across the upland south,
some believe it was brought to Delaware in 1638 by Swedish immigrants; others claim it's a poor man's version of a Georgian manor.
The truth is, no one knows, but it sure is neat.

From there, continue up U.S. Route 167 into **Bernice**, where at a
restaurant/filling station called The Bar-B-Q Place we tanked up then
followed our noses inside. As we delved into delectable brisket sandwiches, owner and chef (as well as mechanic in the adjacent garage)
Gordon Ober was friendly but cagey regarding his homemade mari-
nade, double-cooking technique, and other such alchemy. Can't blame
him. Such tasty secrets are worthy of protection.

North of town is Lynn Creek Winery with tours and tastings of
vintages made from muscadine grapes and—possibly a first—mayhaw
berries. Perhaps vintner Bill will even rouse your interest in his upcoming blends of Louisiana rice wine!

From the downtown light, business district traffic on Louisiana 2
east is slow enough for family dogs to wander carefree, greeting each
other on the sidewalks much like their masters do in the stores. The
Bernice Museum in the old Rock Island depot houses an eclectic collection of local artifacts.

Louisiana 2 toward **Farmerville** is a stretch known for bottle barns.
Why hanging old bottles, of all ages and colors, from the sides of
sheds or the limbs of trees should be this area's chosen mode of artistic expression, no one could tell us. Of **Shiloh**, birthplace of two
Louisiana governors and once home to a Baptist college, little remains but a pair of cemeteries.

The sparkling, watery reaches of Lake Darbonne's State Park offer
camping, nature trails, boat rentals, and a beach beside the fifteen-
thousand-acre fish-stocked reservoir. Just past the lake watch for
Edgewood (private), a 1902 Queen Anne mansion sheltered by trees
off the roadside to the left. Even in obvious disrepair, its magnificent
round porch and fairy-tale turret render it unforgettable. A bit farther,

across Louisiana 2, an ornate three-grave cemetery sports an ivy-covered bower and grieves in marble, "When the music has ended and the rose has gone, like thoughts of a loved one their memory lingers on."

Farmerville's fame these days lies in processing a million chickens a week at the ConAgra plant. Downtown, when Louisiana 2 turns left, continue instead onto Louisiana 15 over a finger of the lake. For the next eighteen miles, chicken barns and Christmas-tree farms punctuate rolling forest. Horses at pasture await their moment of glory in a roadside rodeo arena.

Nearing **Monroe**, Louisiana 15 bumps right for two miles before joining U.S. Route 80. Western stores, flea markets, and seafood restaurants hug the byway into West Monroe's Historic Cottonport District where an impressive row of old storefronts is crowded with antique stores and cafes. Ample parking, ample treasure hunting... Honey, have you got the checkbook?

For more information:

Shreveport/Bossier Tourist Bureau 318-222-9391
    P.O. Box 1761, Shreveport, LA 71166
Caddo-Pine Island Oil Museum 318-995-6845
    200 South Land Avenue, Oil City, LA 71061
Vivian Chamber of Commerce 318-375-5300
    P.O. Box 1, Vivian, LA 71082
Homer Chamber of Commerce 318-927-3271
    519 South Main, Homer, LA 71040
Ford Museum 318-927-9190
    519 South Main, Homer, LA 71040
Germantown Colony & Museum 318-377-4240
    500 Museum Road, Minden, LA 71055
Bonnie & Clyde Trade Days 318-263-2437
    P.O. Box 243, Arcadia, LA 71001
Lincoln Parish/Ruston Visitors Bureau 318-255-2031
    P.O. Box 150, Ruston, LA 71273

Sarah's Kitchen 318-255-1726
    607 Lee Avenue, Ruston, LA 71273
Lincoln Parish Museum/Absalom Autrey House 318-251-0018
    609 North Vienna, Ruston, LA 71273
Lynn Creek Winery 318-285-9298
    1807 Highway 167 North, Bernice, LA 71222
Monroe/West Monroe Visitors Bureau 800-843-1872
    P.O. Box 6054, Monroe, LA 71211-6054

CHAPTER 4
THE LOUISIANA DELTA

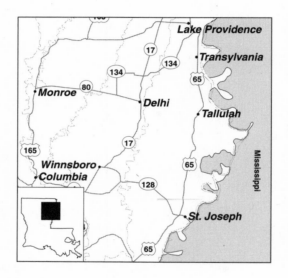

From **MONROE to LAKE PROVIDENCE**, a wide circle south, east, north, and back. About two hundred and thirty miles via Columbia, St. Joseph, and Lake Providence. Features Ouachita River vistas, steamboat towns, Poverty Point prehistoric site, oxbow lakes, and cotton fields ad infinitum. Remember, cotton bolls open just before harvesting begins in mid-September.

South from **Monroe**, U.S. Route 165 finally shrinks to two lanes as suburbs pause in their siege of the Ouachita Valley's cotton-covered flatness. With railroad tracks hugging our left, we kept a sharp eye on the levee flirting at our right. Massed oaks often cache former town sites and antebellum homes. In the distance, we might spot the back of a plantation house, its inviting façade facing the Ouachita River, the main thoroughfare well before the railroad and U.S. Route 165.

Witness to those olden days are privately owned Filhoil Plantation down Logtown School Road and Boscobel Cottage on Cordell Lane. The latter's bed-and-breakfast lodgings include a plantation chapel and newly added dogtrot cabin.

The Ouachita River is kept navigable to modern-day traffic by the Columbia Lock and Dam. For a look at where your taxes go, you can visit this massive piece of engineering, but don't expect to see the locks in action. Traffic is sparse.

During August and September, a tasty four-mile detour, off Blankston Road just south of **Bosco**, is Pender's Pride Muscadine Farm. Buy grapes by the pound, pick them yourself, or, for a dollar, graze the well-tended vines till the tart juice dribbles down your chin.

Orderly rows of pecan trees announce another crop and the first of many such orchards to come. Fall finds roadside stands selling the delectable nuts by the pound. At Riverton Recreation Area, the Caldwell Belle cruises the verdant Ouachita from April to October. An authentic paddle wheeler complete with calliope, a voyage on her re-creates the days when the world possessed no sound more exciting than the steam whistle of a riverboat.

Nearing **Columbia**, a right onto Martin Lane (at the silver tanks of Cordill Propane Service) ambles to the 1878 Martin Homeplace Living History Museum. Inside, home-worn artifacts elicit reveries of times gone by. How painstakingly intricate is an antebellum quilt! Outside, wander among the outbuildings where chickens clucked and hogs grunted or put your hands to a work-worn plow. Unlike grand plantation house tours that show how the "other half" lived, here is a reminder that most nineteenth-century farmers, like most of us today, were of the middle class.

Across the bridge in Columbia proper, a block left leads to Main

Street where antiques and wonderful crafts fill the brick-front shops next to "the oldest saloon on the Ouachita." In the early 1900s, Italian was the language of prosperous merchants along this noisy riverboat landing. One such successful immigrant honored his store with statues of Columbus and Washington. The fancy Schepis Building is now a museum and tourist center. In the other direction, at Main and Church Streets, the magnificent 1911 Scandinavian Gothic First Methodist Church is the town's architectural pinnacle.

The second weekend of October finds scores of traditional and contemporary artists at Columbia's Louisiana Art & Folk Fest. Other times, if you're in luck, Main Street twangs with an outdoor concert by the sheriff's department's country band, The Posse.

Our passion for age-old architecture sent us on an interesting spur to **Clarks**, a sawmill town. Follow U.S. Route 165 south five miles through **Grayson**, with its several flea markets. Turn right onto Louisiana 844 for a mile, then right again on Louisiana 547 south. Looming at the next curve is the Oasis Commissary, a frame structure so large and fantastic it seems a mirage. It now houses the town hall, public library, post office, Masonic Temple, and an air-conditioning contractor.

Just south of Columbia, we turned east off U.S. Route 165 onto Louisiana 849 for a dizzying forty-mile scenic detour. (Granted, "dizzying" is a relative term in Louisiana.) Formerly a Danish farming community, but now open land, Copenhagen Trail roller-coasters through steep hillocks and gorges now guarded by The Nature Conservancy as a preserve for rare plants and marine fossils. This tangle of ravines was once the ocean floor forced up a millennium ago by Mother Nature's leviathan strength.

After nine miles, bear left at the fork onto Louisiana 126. Frequent "Loose Stock Illegal" signs didn't bother a wandering goat herd or cows grazing where they pleased. Even a deer flashed across the road in broad daylight from the forest where hardwoods mingle with the pines in a promise of fall color. Go another ear-popping ten miles, then left onto Louisiana 124 at **Rosefield**, where we dodged an untethered Holstein meticulously weeding the Baptist Church sign. More dramatic terrain helped forgive spots where the pavement gave way to hard-packed gravel, until after six miles we plunged to the tiny Duty Ferry across the Ouachita River. Just in time, our faithful Plymouth rumbled aboard. Rustic houseboats bobbed against the thicketed bank as a storybook tug pushed us to the opposite shore.

Once across, Louisiana 559 north is a mural of river, cypress swamp, moss-draped oaks, and cotton fields until it dead-ends into Louisiana 4. We'd just driven forty miles to get exactly where we'd have been in five miles had we taken Louisiana 4 east directly from Columbia; we didn't regret an inch.

Continuing east on Louisiana 4, ramble through rice fields, then cotton fields, then wooded lowlands and patches of raw prairie. **Winnsboro**, a farm town that boasts of having the "world's largest inland cotton compress," no doubt sires many entrepreneurs as well, for even tiny offices display "We Buy Cotton" signs. Jogging left a block to the Prairie Street Historic District is the newly revamped downtown.

From Winnsboro it's thirty-five lonesome miles through cotton fields and woods, passing few cars and fewer houses, then eastward on Louisiana 128 to **St. Joseph**. This slumbering river town's main street passes beautiful old houses, some Greek Revival, some Italianate, others Victorian. At the Mississippi River, just past the Tensas Parish Library and Museum, go south a few blocks to the 1906 Baroque domed courthouse, Carpenter Gothic church, and more stately vintage homes, all seated sedately around the genteel and unusual New England-village-green-styled square.

Louisiana 605 leaves St. Joseph heading north. A mile out, Louisiana 604 forks between the levee and Lake Bruin, one of the lower Mississippi's many oxbow lakes. Named for their shape, oxbows formed when the fickle river changed course. Abandoned meanderers were cut off to become deep, still lakes. Just off Louisiana 604, Lake Bruin State Park is a tucked away Eden, with swimming, fishing, boat rentals, and primitive camping amid the moss-heavy cypress that edge its shore.

Duty Ferry

Where Louisiana 604 rejoins Louisiana 605, go right, then right again onto Louisiana 608, skirting the southern shore of Lake St. Joseph, yet another oxbow. Here is Winter Quarters, a rambling plantation house that began as a three-room hunting lodge in 1803, the same year these and half a billion adjacent acres joined the United States as the Louisiana Purchase. During the Civil War, its owner's Union sympathies spared Winter Quarters, alone among seventeen Lake St. Joseph mansions, from the torch. Though the house isn't open, stroll its grounds where an enormous sill removed during restoration lies. Few living souls have seen standing cypress trees as big as this house's support beams.

In 1682, the French explorer La Salle paused in his journey down the Mississippi to exchange gifts with the Taensas, a nation whose main village was probably right here on Lake St. Joseph. Researching that expedition's journals for our last book, we'd read how the Taensas king in his fine white robes of soft woven fiber, his wives in their brilliant feathered capes, his slaves and guards and shamans formed a procession dominated by copper disks shimmering high, effigies to the life-giving sun. All this to awe the first white men they had ever seen.

Alas, the journals reveal the jaded Frenchmen were not much impressed.

Backtracking to Louisiana 605, follow the lake to **Newellton**, another picturesque village. Take Louisiana 4 (though The Hideaway Cafe is hidden a block past) out through Newellton toward U.S. Route 65 north, traversing flat croplands to **Tallulah**.

An 1857 railroad town on the Vicksburg, Shreveport and Texas line, Tallulah's greater bequest to transportation came in 1924. A crop-dusting service formed to rid surrounding cotton fields of boll weevils, and thus Delta Airlines got its start. The prettiest part of town is along Walnut Bayou, lined with stately buildings and crossed by sloping foot bridges that summon strollers for a better view. Tallulah has yet to revitalize its downtown, but when the time comes, the marvelous covered arcade at the west end of the business district will be a great start. Imagine the din of heels as shoppers conducted their business sheltered from the weather in this ancestor of the suburban mall.

Tallulah claims two highly popular truck stops as the best cooking around. Located next to each other on U.S. Route 65 south at Interstate 20, from early to late, they offer serious mealtime competition.

The Tensas (TEN-saw) River National Wildlife Refuge near the hamlet of **Quebec** is off U.S. Route 80, west of Tallulah. Here, the endangered Louisiana black bear is making a tenuous comeback. After a stop at the visitors center, venture along the boardwalk into the swampy bottom-land forest's beautiful natural reaches where ruins of an old plantation can still be spotted.

From Tallulah, U.S. Route 65 north is arrow-straight, and the land is billiard-table-flat except where the serpentine Mississippi pushes its levee into view across the fertile delta's cotton fields. We rejoiced in the relief provided by the rare house dotting the horizon, the occasional pecan grove with roadside stand awaiting fall sales, or the couple of country stores.

One of those stores in **Transylvania** fills its shelves with vampire souvenirs, trading on its name. Of course, Dracula's Transylvania is far away in eastern Europe; and the legendary creature this area did give us is much more historic anyway. In a nearby backwater slough, President Theodore ("Teddy") Roosevelt refused to shoot a trophy of a black bear when its cub happened from the woods (or so one version of the story goes). The incident garnered national publicity and inspired the beloved "teddy bear."

Nearing **Lake Providence**, restaurants and stores materialize. Minsky's Pecan Market stocks an assortment of local food products and pecan varieties in season. Winding into downtown finds the heavenly Mennonite-run Ole Dutch Bakery. Ten tables and a tempting menu make it a popular lunch spot, but what hooked us was the scent of cinnamon and poppy-seed breads. Buy enough for the road and home, or you'll just wind up turning around and going back as we did.

Once a boisterous river town, in 1833 Providence (so named because it took an act of providence for flatboat crews to make it this far past river pirates) shifted its face to the south shore of a nearby oxbow lake. U.S. Route 65 outlines its bank where cypress trees step down into the water. Noticing a fair-sized mud flat, we blinked as it sailed skyward in a thunder of flapping wings, revealing itself to be an enormous flock of wild ducks.

Among the dozen or so fine old mansions facing the lake, the Byerley House offers directions to the historic district and regional information. From its Victorian porch, you can spy the remains of a canal General Ulysses Grant dug in a failed attempt to sneak his gun boats around the Confederate canons at Vicksburg. Locals still recount how the back-breaking canal work killed even the unit's roughest, toughest sergeant, and how "he turned out to be... a she." A staunch abolitionist from a Kansas cow town had disguised herself to fight for the Union cause.

Farther on, a couple of motel-restaurants offer lake swimming, while the new Louisiana Cotton Museum halfway between them features the story of the South's king crop. Back near town, Louisiana 134 traces Tensas Bayou west curving alongside ancient swales of the Mississippi.

Just past Bayou Maçon (MAY-sun), a right onto Louisiana 577 goes to Poverty Point Commemorative Area. Here, expansive, enigmatic earthworks mark what many believe was North America's largest city... three thousand years ago. Now three millennia is quite a long time, so there are more questions than answers about who lived here. Standing atop the giant bird-shaped mound, it's impossible not to wonder: Why was this built? Was Poverty Point inhabited year round or reserved as a seasonal religious site or as a trading center? In a time before established agriculture, how did so many people in one place feed themselves?

Some things are known. No matter how out of the way Poverty Point might seem to the modern traveler, in prehistoric, pre-levee times, its location made great sense. Atop the Maçon Ridge, this lone finger of terrace in the broad Mississippi flood plain was safe from even the worst inundations.

The artifacts in the interpretive center impress as much by their quantity as their age. Indeed, farmers plowed right over these mounds, turning up artifacts, for decades before aerial photography revealed just how extensive the site is. With two miles of walking trails, a thorough visit can take two hours.

From Poverty Point take Louisiana 134 south to U.S. Route 17 into **Delhi** (Dell-HIGH) where W.C. Thomson Drugs' soda counter and lunch booths are the combined meeting spot for the older locals. Settling in for a coke float and hand-blended shake, we inquired about rumors we'd heard of outlaws in the area.

"Jesse James! Had a sister lived here," brightened one senior.

"Was a girlfriend!" interrupted another.

"Whatever, he'd visit her. Was a tunnel from her house to the bayou—his escape! So whenever'd the law come..."

We smiled and settled in to listen.

U.S. Route 80 cruises west through "white gold" (cotton) country. From Rayville to Monroe, the road runs straight, but the terrain is varied: fields and meadow, deep cypress swamp, and rows of pecan trees. River crossings intersperse small towns. A village named "Start" inspires interesting signs, including "Start Elementary School" and "Start Tree Trimming". But sadly this was the end, not the start, of our journey.

For more information:

Monroe-West Monroe Visitors Bureau 800-843-1872
    1333 State Farm Drive, Monroe, LA 71202

Boscobel Cottage Bed and Breakfast 318-325-1550
    185 Cordell Lane, Monroe, LA 71202

Caldwell Belle Paddlewheeler 318-649-2138
    P.O. Box 10, Columbia, LA 71418

Columbia Chamber of Commerce 318-649-2138
    P.O. Box 10, Columbia, LA 71418

Madison Parish/Tallulah Chamber of Commerce 318-574-2662
    Route 2, Box 88, Mound, LA 71282

Tensas River National Wildlife Refuge 318-574-2664
    Route 2, Box 295, Tallulah, LA 71282

Byerly House/ Lake Providence
    Chamber of Commerce 318-559-5125
    600 Lake Street, U.S. Route 65 North,
    Lake Providence, LA 71254

Ole Dutch Bakery 318-559-1574
    208 Lake Street, Lake Providence, LA 71254

Poverty Point State Commemorative Area 318-926-5492
    P.O. Box 276, Epps, LA 71237

CHAPTER 5
THE COLONIAL TRAIL

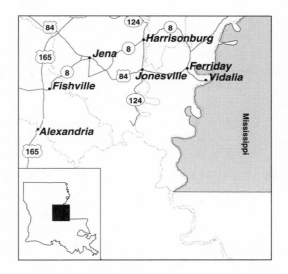

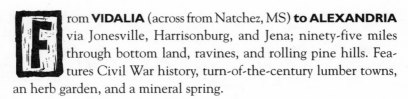 rom **VIDALIA** (across from Natchez, MS) **to ALEXANDRIA** via Jonesville, Harrisonburg, and Jena; ninety-five miles through bottom land, ravines, and rolling pine hills. Features Civil War history, turn-of-the-century lumber towns, an herb garden, and a mineral spring.

Vidalia has always been a rugged border town, the place Natchez planters went to settle arguments with pistols. Jim Bowie almost didn't make his date with destiny at the Alamo, so badly was he once mauled in a Vidalia free-for-all. Nowadays, Vidalia feeds on Natchez's casino traffic with cheaper motels and less-taxed liquor. Drive-thru barns for spirits are almost as common as drive-thru windows for fast food along Vidalia's U.S. Route 84 strip.

For heartier fare, try the Sandbar Restaurant at the foot of the bridge or the West Bank Eatery north on Levee Road, which also offers a river view. And for grander accommodations, turn right from U.S. Route 84 onto Highway 3196 where Lisburn Hall, an 1852 Greek Revival plantation bed and breakfast, overlooks Lake Concordia.

With barely a rural break, U.S. Route 84 enters **Ferriday**, birthplace of Jerry Lee Lewis, Jimmy Swaggart, Mickey Gilley, and Howard K. Smith, thus providing America with sins, sermons, songs, and sober newscasts. At a traffic light that only makes it to 6:00 P.M. before dozing off to flashing yellow, a left kept us on U.S. Route 84 through woods fighting with cotton fields carved from the northern reaches of the huge Dismal Swamp. This road has a long history. Often called the Colonial Trail, sometimes simply "the Texas Road," it was a route east for fattened cattle and west for hungry adventurers. At least we were going in the right direction.

Seven miles from Ferriday, Frogmore Plantation (private) is almost overshadowed by a tree-topped Indian mound a hundred yards past it.

Crossing the Tensas River into **Jonesville**, turn right at the foot of the bridge, then right again to Champlin Net Company. Here is a store devoted entirely to the fisherman, but not your average weekend trout sleuth. Commercial fishing, especially catfishing, is big business in this town where four rivers meet. If you're in need of mud boots or rain gear of any size this is the place to buy 'em. Champlin sells more kinds of nets, traps, and gear than you ever knew existed. But the staff enjoys explaining, and if your timing's right, you may catch them actually making nets.

Down the block, an early 1900s cemetery climbs an Indian mound and Four Rivers Park straddles a flood wall. First Street leads past old brick storefronts and sheet-metal cotton gins to Louisiana 124. A right turn over Little River Bridge starts you past catfish ponds and turtle farms toward Harrisonburg. The road offers some pretty views of the lower Ouachita River, its flood plain dotted with Indian mounds that rise unexpectedly from the flat terrain.

A historical marker in Jonesville claims the site of Anilco, an Indian town and eighty-foot-high temple mound praised by the 1540s de Soto expedition as having "much corn, beans, walnuts and persimmons, the most populous of any country." Many historians argue Anilco was actually hundreds of miles north. Regardless, this area was definitely settled well before de Soto ever got his boots muddy on the continent.

Louisiana 124 joins Louisiana 8 beside a steep gravestone-studded hill at quaint **Harrisonburg**. Curl around the courthouse to the 1853 Methodist Church. Pocked with bullet holes, they're mementos of when this strategic bluff overlooking the Ouachita was traded back and forth during the Civil War. Take Short Street from the church, turning right on Sicily and left on Catahoula to the old Sargeant Hotel, once a hopping steamboat inn. Louisiana 124 (Duty Ferry Road) climbs the pine-covered hill toward Veterans Memorial Park and the historic site of Confederate Fort Beauregard before continuing fifteen miles to the ferry crossing taken in Chapter 4.

From Harrisonburg, Louisiana 8 west rides the cusp where flat lands to the left morph into hillside forests on the right for most of the twenty-five miles to **Jena** (JEEN-uh).

Jena's slip of businesses is a good place to grab a bite. Two miles past downtown on U.S. Route 84, a left turn just past the hospital leads to LaSalle Parish Museum. Housed in the 1906 Good Pine & Tall Timber Lumber Company building, it has remarkably wide porches with a petrified tree in front. A dozen nearby homes date from when this suburb of Jena was a company town.

South on Louisiana 773, the Belah Store and Museum invites sightseers for a soda, a sweet, and a look at the fine collection of accumulated artifacts. Citizens around here pride themselves on remembering the old ways. The December Colonial Trail Days Festival revives folkways such as old-time syrup making. From a press powered by a

Dogwood Blossoms

circle-plodding mule and a hot fire of "fat pine," eight hundred stalks of cane squeeze into three barrels of juice that cook down to a dozen gallons of syrup. Darling, put the biscuits on!

Leaving Jena on Louisiana 8 west, pine trees close in around us, freshening the air. Cut into an isolated clearing, Eden Methodist Church may seem unremarkable but, established in 1788, it's one of the oldest Protestant church sites west of the Mississippi.

A rare cluster of oil-field drilling derricks have been left standing in a pasture, almost as if the roughnecks just stepped away for lunch.

On the right, scattered picnic tables and a replica gazebo mark the site of White Sulphur Springs, a turn-of-the-century health resort famous for hydropathy. The "curative" mineral waters still flow from a spring under the gazebo and still carry the telltale bad-egg smell of sulphur.

Such subtle attractions carried us into Kisatchie National Forest toward the hamlet of **Fishville**. Just before the Big Creek bridge and the Fishville store, watch for Ridgaway Herb Gardens & Tea Room. Call ahead to arrange for a scrumptious tea with gracious chef extraordinaire, Jean Owen. You can buy plants by the shovelful or simply stroll through the bucolic rows of foliage as Jean breaks off bits of herbs, each a surprise to nose or palate. "This one makes a soothing tea," she explains. "This one is perfect for flavoring pasta sauce." This beautiful, tranquil locale makes it obvious why Fishville was once the premier getaway spot for Alexandrians.

Louisiana 8 enters **Pollock** where the bright Indian Inn offers a hearty plate lunch. Jogging right, Louisiana 8 passes a sumptuous Victorian house on the way to **Bentley** (and Chapter 6). Mid-March to mid-April, if the day is bright, take U.S. Route 165 north to Forest Service Road 120 where the Kisatchie Dogwood Auto Tour explores ten miles of pine forest aglow with white blossoms.

But this day our goal was **Alexandria**, a dozen miles south on U.S. Route 165. The city that locals call Alex overflows with seldom-heralded charms. (We never knew they had brick streets!)

The classiest place to stay in Alex, arguably in all Louisiana, is Main Street's Hotel Bentley. Built in 1908, its elegance remains breathtaking. The lobby alone, with its cathedral-like ceilings and faux-Persian-carpet mosaic tile floor, leaves little wonder why, when in 1940 America held its largest ever peacetime maneuvers here, it was at the Bentley that generals, including Eisenhower, chose to stay. So we end the chapter ogling the same opulence that Ike, himself a farm boy, ogled more than a half century ago.

For more information:

Vidalia/State Welcome Center 318-336-7008
    1401 Carter Street, Vidalia 71375
Lisburn Hall Bed and Breakfast 800-972-0127
    P.O. Box 1152, Vidalia, LA 71313
Harrisonburg/Sargeant Hotel Visitors Info 318-744-5794
    P.O. Box 320, Harrisonburg, LA 71340
Grant Parish Tourist Commission 318-765-3161
    P.O. Box 357, Pollock, LA 71467
Ridgaway Herb Gardens and Tea Room 318-765-9294
    Route 1, Box 810, Pollock, LA 71467
Kisatchie National Forest
    Catahoula Ranger District 318-765-3554
    5325 Louisiana Highway 8, Bentley, LA 71407
Hotel Bentley 800-356-6835
    200 Desoto Street, Alexandria, LA 71301
Alexandria-Pineville Visitors Bureau 318-443-7049
    P.O. Box 8110, Alexandria, LA 71306

CHAPTER 6
PINE TREES
AND POLITICS

 LEXANDRIA to RUSTON via Winnfield and Jonesboro. Features a historical log village, pine vistas, a Passion Play, and the birthplaces of four colorful governors. About a hundred miles.

From Alexandria, U.S. Route 167 crosses the Red River to Pineville, then curves north to the quiet burg of **Bentley**. Well, quiet except for the sawing and hammering from Trader's Rendez-Vous Frontier Village, just east on Louisiana 8. Many folks collect antiques. Farm implements? Hey, even we have an old plow decorating our lawn. But the Thorne family at Trader's Rendez-Vous also collects buildings—one-room log cabins and cow barns. And wagons, sturdy stock wagons and jaunty surreys. And wells. Syrup mills. A blacksmith shop. How'd they ever move that grindstone in? And how'd they get all this stuff working again? Surrounded by a log palisade, the outcome is an 1800s frontier theme park without the rides. So hitch your steed, mosey on in, and see what the Thornes are up to.

After Trader's Rendez-Vous, hills and pine trees undulate endlessly northward along U.S. Route 167 toward Winnfield. This is the Kisatchie National Forest Catahoula Ranger District. In **Williana**, spurs onto Forest Road 472 and Louisiana 155 lead to woodland campsites often tucked near a bayou or dogwood grove.

Winnfield welcomes you with antique shops and signs to the popular Southern Colonial bed and breakfast, a 1908 inn. Over a bridge and across the tracks, you'll find Main Street east of, and parallel to, U.S. Route 167. Its storefronts are still occupied with offices, shops, even a restaurant. The old depot hosts a trio of museums, one devoted to local history, another to forestry. The third is the Louisiana Political Museum and Hall of Fame.

Winnfield is birthplace to three twentieth-century Louisiana governors. The most famous, Huey Long, has been portrayed in the movies by Ed Asner, John Goodman, and (in a fictionalized version) Broderick Crawford. No slight to those fine actors, but Huey himself was much the better performer. Derided as a clown yet despised as a dictator, labeled a Communist by the Right and a Fascist by the Left, he'd nevertheless become a rival to FDR before being assassinated in 1935. Whatever his faults, Huey built hospitals, bridges, and many of the roads traveled in this book.

Governor Earl Long, Huey's little brother, served multiple terms, but they were tainted by scandal over his romance with a strip-tease artist and interrupted by a stint in a mental asylum. When they made the movie about Earl, he was played by Paul Newman.

Winnfield's third native-son governor never got a movie. O.K. Allen was Huey's hand-picked successor, much to the dismay of Earl.

His initials (for Oscar Kelly) were appropriate to a governor so accommodating he reputedly once signed a leaf blown onto his desk through an open window.

Main Street leads east past pretty Victorian homes to Earl K. Long Park and home site. After greeting Uncle Earl's statue, wander back to U.S. Route 167 to continue north.

Starting in 1840, the more fertile parts of these piney hills were cleared for cotton by settlers moving west from the Appalachian piedmont. Folks claim that in out-of-the-way corners of the area you can still hear traces of their cadenced Scotch-Irish brogue. In the twentieth century, thin soils and boll weevils ended cotton farming, but even before that, the deepest woods were infamous for harboring outlaws like the Sparta Road Nightriders and the 1870s Kimbrell Gang of Coochie Brake whose murderous ways would chill even Jesse James.

In **Jonesboro**, the Courthouse sits on Jimmie Davis Boulevard, once called Main Street— a good omen since it's Jimmie Davis's stomping ground we're bound for. Jonesboro's brochure touts itself as a place "where there's nothing to do... but relax." It's not far from true. There are a few antique shops, cafes, and a local museum. For trivia fans, there's also what Guiness declares the world's longest sidewalk. Leading two miles to **Hodge**, it's a path for workers who keep the world's largest kraft-paper machine belching out grocery bags by the kazillion.

The White Oak Restaurant at U.S. Route 167 and West Third Street in **North Hodge** is a ten-table hot spot for Southern cooking careening toward soul food. Know how chain cafeterias measure each portion they serve? At the White Oak, they measure you, look you up and down, decide how hungry you seem, and fill your plate accordingly. Is the food good? Ask the cook who'll joyfully reply, "Add a little pepper, some onion on the side, and you'll be sitting high, slapping ante!"

Stay on U.S. Route 167 north out of Hodge. At **Punkin Center** (sic), just past the well-stocked Looking Back Antique Flea Market, turn right on Louisiana 811 (Gladway Road) for three miles, then left on Louisiana 542 to the Jimmie Davis Tabernacle.

Set among a few rural homes in the middle of nowhere, the immense A-frame church with giant colored panes reaches above the pine-tree tops. Next to it is Jimmie's weathered board-and-batten four-room birthplace. Across the road is the Peckerwood General Store. A cement stage and electrical hookups remind us that a small city rises here during occasional gospel revivals.

In case you don't know—and haven't guessed—Jimmie Davis was a governor of Louisiana in the mid-1940s, then back for an encore in 1960 when he beat Earl Long. But Jimmie's greater fame, what won him induction into the Country Music Hall of Fame, was his career as singer/songwriter.

Both the words and musical notation to the opening bars of his greatest hit, "You Are My Sunshine" (after which he named one of the state's larger bridges), are centered on Jimmie's headstone in the family graveyard behind the tabernacle. This pink slab of granite is even bigger than that grindstone back at Trader's Rendez-Vous. Its inscribed face begins with a three-foot copy of Jimmie's signature and ends with his terms of office as governor. Prior, lesser offices are carved onto the back. Only two things are missing from this extraordinary sepulcher: One is a closing date, and the other is Jimmie himself—for when this book went to press, he was still very much alive, but obviously planning ahead.

Like Huey and Earl Long, Jimmie Davis had a movie made about him, but he didn't trust just any old actor to carry off the role. Jimmie himself went off to Hollywood to star in the opus about a hillbilly singer who becomes governor of Louisiana.

In 1985, when Glen was preparing to direct a movie, Jimmie Davis auditioned. He was good, but he was also eighty-four years old. Perhaps the rigors of the shoot would be too much. Glen gave the part to somebody else. A decade later, long after the film in question had had its run in theaters, on cable, and on the late late show, finding its way to the back corner of the video store, Jimmie Davis was still playing gigs, singing in his same steady baritone, cracking jokes between songs. Oh well, if 'ifs' were skiffs, we'd all be poling down the bayou.

From the Tabernacle, continue on Louisiana 542 to **Quitman**, then head north on U.S. Route 167 to **Clay**. The settlement's two cotton gins are long gone, and its fields grown up in loblolly pine, but Clay General Store sports a few local artifacts alongside merchandise on the age-worn shelving, making it a good soda stop.

Just south of **Ruston** summer and early fall evenings find folks crowding into an outdoor theater for the Louisiana Passion Play. A huge cast depicts major events in the life of Christ with a dramatic performance that harkens back to medieval pageants.

Old-time religion seems to thrive amongst pine trees, floating easy on the scented air like a Jimmie Davis hymn.

For more information:

Grant Parish Tourist Commission 318-765-3161
    P.O. Box 357, Pollock, LA 71467
Trader's Rendez-Vous Frontier Village 318-899-5454
    P.O. Box 68, Bentley, LA 71407
Southern Colonial Bed and Breakfast 318-628-6087
    801 East Main Street, Winnfield, LA 71483
Louisiana Political Museum 318-628-5928
    499 East Main Street, Winnfield, LA 71483
Winn Parish/Winnfield Chamber of Commerce 318-628-4461
    P.O. Box 565, Winnfield, LA 71483
Jackson/Jonesboro Chamber of Commerce 318-259-4693
    P.O. Box 220, Jonesboro, LA 71251
Louisiana Passion Play 318-255-6277
    3010 South Vienna, Ruston, LA 71270
Lincoln Parish/Ruston Chamber of Commerce 318-255-2031
    P.O. Box 150, Ruston, LA 71273

CHAPTER 7

THE NORTH SHORE

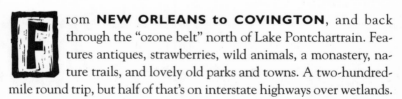

rom **NEW ORLEANS to COVINGTON**, and back
through the "ozone belt" north of Lake Pontchartrain. Features antiques, strawberries, wild animals, a monastery, nature trails, and lovely old parks and towns. A two-hundred-
mile round trip, but half of that's on interstate highways over wetlands.

From New Orleans, Interstate 10 west brushes through feathery cypress treetops and over the LaBranche wetlands to nip the edge of
Lake Pontchartrain. Switch to Interstate 55 north to climb the wild
isthmus between that lake and its little sister, Maurepas. Exit on U.S.

Route 51, the parallel "old highway," at **Manchac**.

Ancient Tangipahoa Indian middens of oyster and clam shells border Pass Manchac which connects the two lakes. From here, Europeans commanded the short-cut water route from the Mississippi River near Baton Rouge to Lake Pontchartrain and the Gulf. By 1900, cypress lumbering was the draw. On west-bound flights from New Orleans International, you can still see the bicycle-spoke scars of pullboat runs that hauled timber from the swamp. Today, tour boats ply the waterways. Manchac's attraction above all is fresh seafood, seasoned, boiled, or fried, at Middendorf's Restaurant.

Follow U.S. Route 51 north seven miles (in spring, past purple and yellow roadside iris and spidery white swamp asters) to the Joyce Wildlife Management Area. A small kiosk marks its thousand-foot boardwalk through the croaking swamp and rustling marsh.

After Joyce, U.S. Route 51 flows into Interstate 55. At the second Ponchatoula exit, go left on Louisiana 22 west across the Yellow Water River Bridge to Taste of Bavaria Bakery. This cozy cafe serves copious Bavarian breakfasts, lunch specials, and scrumptious pastries and breads that will have you plotting your return before you leave.

The famous Kliebert's Alligator Farm lies north on Yellow Water Road, and Ponchatoula's many antique shops are just east, but on our early-morning jaunt neither were yet open, so happy but heavier we doubled back under Interstate 55 to U.S. Route 51 Business the few miles north to **Hammond**.

Once a Confederate shoemaking center, Hammond's early-1900s downtown boomed as a shipping point for rough lumber and delicate strawberries. Now an interstate crossroads and college town, the Victorian-era downtown still bustles, and passengers still board the *City of New Orleans* at the Queen Anne Revival depot.

East on Charles Street, past the 1899 Gothic First Methodist Church, the huge Peter Hammond Oak shields the bones of the adventurous Swedish sailor who quit the sea to render local pine trees into pitch and tar. The last block of Charles is high-tone "Banker's Row." Its 1906 Preston House is particularly impressive with ornate banisters, arched windows, and glassed cupola. A block north, Robert Street leads west past block after oak-lined block of fine old 1920s bungalows. At the deadend, jog right to Church Street which zooms into busy U.S. Route 190.

Beyond a few antique shops and edge-of-town motels lies **Albany**, the 1890s transport point for local Hungarian strawberry growers. Stores with Magyar names commemorate settlers who turned cut-over timber lands into glistening strawberry fields. South on Louisiana 43, an old church remains from Arapadon, once America's largest rural Hungarian settlement.

From mid-March through early May, produce stalls border U.S. Route 51 north. Fat, red strawberries are sold by the flat, a cardboard crate of a dozen pint baskets. Their shelf life—even out of the heat—is a couple of days. Refrigeration or freezing extends the life but reduces the flavor. But since Louisiana strawberries are melt-in-your-mouth sweeter than the California strawberries the rest of the nation must settle for, a flat can disappear mighty quickly. Indulge!

Want strawberries with a longer shelf life? Stop at the Black Cat Grocery between **Tickfaw** and **Independence** for some locally produced Amato Strawberry Wine, available in four varieties from dry to old-fashioned sweet.

Strawberries drew so many Italians to Independence, it's still called "Little Italy" and its restaurants feature Italian specialties. Most of the historic store fronts, built after a 1913 fire, bear Italian names. Even one that doesn't, Klotzbach's Bakery, offers yeasty Italian bread in a half dozen shapes and sizes. The elaborate St. Joseph's Day Procession in March and the music-filled Italian Festival in April are ideal times to visit.

U.S. Route 51 continues to **Amite** where bed and breakfasts abound. But we crossed the tracks onto Louisiana 40, a piney, farm-dotted road that leads to Zemurray Gardens. Open only when spring blooms tremble with color, these flower-brilliant gardens feature walking and driving paths encircling a lake.

At the Global Wildlife Center, a thousand exotic and endangered animals mingle on a square mile of pasture. Minus any carnivores, the giraffes and camels happily mosey amidst Watusi steer, water buffalo, Sika deer, and dozens of other species in a surreal peaceable kingdom. Exotic heads poke snuffing noses into the covered wagon whenever the ninety-minute tour pauses to pass out treats. It's like a Disney movie!

If the Wildlife Center's critters seem pampered to you, keep driving; this area also boasts a multimillion-dollar horse industry. Pedigreed colts romp in pastures all the way to **Folsom**, where Louisiana 40 butts into Louisiana 25.

Most times of year, we'd say turn right. But if it's the third week in October, get thee north past wholesale nurseries, dairy farms, and pine trees to **Franklinton**. Azaleas along driveways and dogwood hiding in the forest await spring, but what people hereabouts eye the calendar for is the Washington Parish Free Fair, an annual autumnal tradition since 1911.

From the Wednesday morning home-grown parade to the last note of the country star-spangled Saturday-night concert, this honest-to-goodness old-time country fair features a midway, home cooking, livestock competitions, bakeoffs, pig-calling contests, husband-calling contests, you name it. The extensive fairgrounds feature the permanent 1800s-era Mile Branch Settlement, alive with school marms and blacksmiths. Even though folks spend the whole year perfecting their blue-ribbon talents, the excitement ends on Saturday because Sunday is church day for this down-home community.

Back in Folsum, Louisiana 25 goes south to **Covington**. En route, take River Road to St. Joseph Abbey. Crossing the steep banks of Bogue Falaya, a one-lane bridge enters the hushed, almost-century-old Benedictine monastery that still houses a hundred monks and seminarians. Stroll to the church where Belgian monk Dom de Witt's extensive 1940s murals combine European inspirational painting with exuberant American celebrate-the-common-man panache—as if God and His saints descended onto a Depression-era WPA post-office mural!

Continuing on River Road, amble through the dappled woods to Lee Road (Louisiana 437). Where Lee merges into U.S. Route 190, take a hard right (staying on Louisiana 437) for two blocks before turning left onto Columbia Street. Entering Covington's thriving downtown historic district, you'll pass artists' studios and antique shops.

Near the major intersection of Boston Street is H.J. Smith's Son, a throwback to the days when a good hardware store had wood floors and sold everything from crockery to nails. This one has taken that rule even further to include a gosh-darn amazing museum of antique machines, an enormous dugout skiff, a scary lead coffin, and lots more.

As head of navigation on the Bogue Falaya and Tchefuncte River, Covington grew from a 1769 British West Florida settlement into a bustling port. Sailing schooners off-loaded freight onto ox carts for Covington merchants and farmsteads. A unique feature of the town's design is found in the ox yards in the center of each downtown block.

Covington is still abustle with tea rooms, restaurants, and a lovely park on the Bogue Falaya. Antique and gift shops teem along Lee Lane. Walking tour info and other brochures are available at many spots.

Follow Boston Street east to Louisiana 36 and into **Abita Springs**. Across from the Scandinavian Gothic Lutheran Church is the Abita Cafe, the local gathering spot for breakfast and sandwiches. A lion-headed spigot at the Abita Springs Tourist Park still spews the mineral-laced spring water that gave the town its fame. A Victorian pavilion recalls the days when working-class New Orleanians excursioned here by train to partake of the healthful "Ozone Belt," a nickname bestowed for the pure, pine-scented air. Behind the pavilion is a section of the Tammany Trace, a defunct railroad right-of-way transformed into a walking, biking, and jogging path through deep woods and over old trestles.

Outside the park, the Abita Brew Pub is the perfect spot to settle in for a nosh, pick up cool gifts, and enjoy some of the best and most

Preston House

inventive suds in the South. Ask about their seasonal beers, the ro-
tating Brewer's Choice, and their root beer. Tours and tastings are
held at the actual brewery a mile west on Louisiana 36.

Beside the pub, Louisiana 59 leads south to **Mandeville** and the
choppy blue waters of Lake Pontchartrain. Houses and ancient oaks
along Lake Shore Drive have been a favorite getaway from the hub-
bub of New Orleans for centuries. But while you're encouraged to
stroll the pleasant lakeside park, picnics are seriously forbidden.

Restaurants on the lake offer great views and tasty dishes. Upscale
Bechac's was an 1800s gambling spot, quite fitting since this land was
once part of Bertrand Marigny de Mandeville's plantation. A dashing
figure who won and gambled away fortunes with a flick of the wrist,
he introduced craps to America. Mandeville is also decision time!
Which of three routes to take back to New Orleans?

The simplest is the Causeway, at twenty-six miles the world's longest bridge. From its middle, you can't see land in any direction, certainly a change of pace after a day's sightseeing. It is also the easiest route. Simply follow Monroe Street (four blocks back from the lake) west.

Or go a few blocks farther from the lake to U.S. Route 190. To the east, just over Bayou Castine, the Northlake Nature Center's well-marked paths meander through sun-dappled, green-washed swamp. Two miles farther, Fontainebleau State Park cradles ruins of Marigny's 1829 sugar plantation and an alley of lake-blown live oaks.

In **Lacombe**, a museum a block north on 12th Street details poet/missionary Abbe Roquette's life among the local Choctaw. Seventh Street bumps four miles through reeds and weeds to Lake Pontchartrain. Birds yakked at our car, and a wild mink that zipped across our path couldn't have been more startled than we were. But at the end of the road, the view is beautiful, with a lone camp on stilts over the water and, when we were there, a gusty breeze teasing the lake with scattered whitecaps.

Tucked in the woods east of Lacombe is the Indian Hills nudist camp, a naturalist's retreat among the pines. Then comes **Slidell**, an 1881 railroad town and now the zenith of northshore suburban sprawl. Coming in on U.S. Route 190, a right after the tracks leads to Olde Towne Slidell's old jail museum, boutiques, and soda shop, all on First Street within walking distance of City Hall.

Slidell is the gateway to historic Fort Pike to the south, the scenic Bogue Chitto National Wildlife Refuge to the north, and Honey Island Swamp to the east where tours unveil some of the state's most pristine wetlands. Had your fill? Front Street is also U.S. Route 11, which leads south over an arm of Lake Pontchartrain into New Orleans.

Finally, should you choose to go west from Mandeville, follow U.S. Route 190 through the thickening congestion of New Orleans's more fashionable suburbs. Eventually, the road escapes to Fairview State Park's historic Otis House sandwiched in a lazy bend of the shady

Tchefuncte River.

The inviting restaurants of **Madisonville** front the river. Back when it was called Coquille, French for "shell" from local clam-shell middens, this was the lake's principal northshore port. It was also the starting point of the forest trace to Natchez and thence to Nashville, a five-hundred-mile footpath for the "Kaintucks" who'd safely guided their flatboats down the Ohio and Mississippi past river pirates, only to brave forest bandits on the long walk home.

On the left, marshland stretches, with a lake view featuring an old sentry lighthouse. Right, Main Street winds past Victorian and Creole cottages to Poole Mansion, a huge 1911 timber baron's palace, now a posh interior-design showroom. Across from it down Rampart Street, the Madisonville Museum inhabits the old courthouse and jail. Even if it's closed, go around back for a sobering view of the cells.

Just past Poole Mansion, turn left onto Johnson Street, which soon winds to a country lane known as Old Ponchatoula Highway. Where it meets its replacement, Louisiana 22, a right starts the wooded drive (a deer ran across the road!) to the dozens of antique stores of **Ponchatoula**. After a day of sightseeing, we were ready to loosen our gams and hunt for treasure.

Ponchatoula heralds itself both as "Strawberry Capital" and "America's Antique City," having effected an amazing revitalization by converting its once-shuttered storefronts to antique shops, cafes, and country markets. The sidewalks were crowded. Accents marked visitors as north Louisianians or down-the-bayou Cajuns. Had the accents been Hungarian, Italian, or with a Scots brogue, we might have been back amidst Ponchatoula's turn-of-the-century bustle.

Back onto Interstate 55 south, we raced the sun across the swamps to end the day behind a mountain of boiled crabs at Middendorf's in Manchac. Writing guidebooks is hard, but someone's got to do it.

For more information:

Tangipahoa Parish Tourist Commission 504-542-7520
42271 South Morrison Boulevard, Hammond, LA 70433
Taste of Bavaria Bakery & Restaurant 504-386-3634
14476 Louisiana 22, Ponchatoula, LA 70454
Kliebert Alligator Farm (March - October) 504-345-3617
41067 West Yellow Water Road, Hammond, LA 70401
Hammond Chamber of Commerce 504-345-4457
P.O. Drawer 1458, Hammond, LA 70404
Zemurray Gardens 504-878-2284
23115 Zemurray Gardens Drive, Loranger, LA 70446
Global Wildlife Center 504-624-WILD
26389 Highway 40, Folsom, LA 70437
Franklinton Chamber of Commerce 504-839-5822
100 Main Street, Franklinton, LA 70438
Covington Downtown Development Commission 504-892-1873
P.O. Box 778, Covington, LA 70434
St. Tammany Parish Tourist Commission 800-634-9443
600 North Highway 190, Suite 15, Covington, LA 70433
Abita Brewing Company 800-737-2311
72011 Holly Street, Abita Springs, LA 70420
Ponchatoula Chamber of Commerce 504-386-2533

CHAPTER 8

UP THE BAYOU

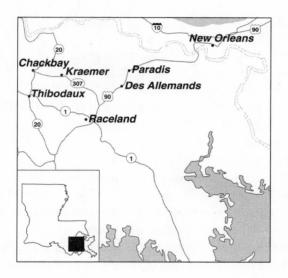

 rom **NEW ORLEANS to THIBODAUX**, a hundred and twenty miles round trip through wetlands and along the sugar country of Bayou Lafourche, with swamp tours, plantation villages, and the many attractions of Thibodaux.

Out of New Orleans on Interstate 10 west hop on Interstate 310 to swoop over the swamps and across the river and through the sugar cane and into the woods. This is the overture, a taste of the landscapes our route will later digest at leisure. Land and water war, with water usually winning. Rows of cane stand boastfully straight, but it takes man, busy man, to keep the jungle from bullying them aside.

At **Des Allemands** (duh ZAL-munz) veer right onto Louisiana 631 to amble through the village. Des Allemands (the name means Germans, after early settlers) grew with antebellum railways that made it subject to Civil War attacks as rebel guerrillas grew adept at ambushing trains. Its namesake bayou links Lac des Allemands upstream to Lake Salvador downstream. Wind along the narrow waterfront lanes where piled nets and crab traps teeter on the bayou's edge as families clean the day's catch. To taste the local specialty, catfish, cross over the bridge back onto U.S. Route 90. Well past town is Spahr's Restaurant, known far and wide for copious portions of crisp-fried seafood. Don't let its gas station facade deter you.

Surrounding swamps squeeze U.S. Route 90, threatening to take back this strip of wetlands that was first dug up then filled back in to build the roadway in 1919. An occasional break in the undergrowth reveals a heron rookery, cattle grazing, or stretches of marsh crisscrossed by boats skimming along canals.

Follow Swamp Tour signs onto Louisiana 3199 then cut north on Louisiana 307, crossing Bayou Boeuf to follow Bayou L'Ours west. The former bayou name (applied to many state streams, with varying pronunciation; here it's "buff") implies that colonial explorers spotted buffalo grazing on the banks; the latter bayou name means bear. While you're not likely to see bears and certainly no buffalo, both deer and alligators create occasional road hazards, so drive carefully.

In the mood for a swamp tour? In **Kraemer** are two of the most popular in the state. Both Zam's and Torres's tours are run by died-in-the-seafood-boil bayou Cajuns. The keen eye of Torres opens up the mysterious swamp like a friendly book, coupling a down-home attitude with knowledge earned through years as a Fish and Game Agent. His backyard is a small zoo.

Zam's explores basically the same route, along Bayou Boeuf through the backwater swamps of the basin trapped between the Mississippi River and Bayou Lafourche. On account of Zam's fur and alligator buying businesses, you'll see lots of skins hung out to dry as well as gator-head souvenirs in his gift shop.

In the 1890s, an international fad for alligator shoes, traveling bags, and even upholstery created a hunting boom. By the 1960s, ever-rarer alligators finally won federal protection. Their spectacular come-back in the wild coupled with a profusion of alligator farms has made them big business again, though a newer fad often makes the meat more valuable than the hide.

Edwina's Restaurant, next to Zam's, specializes in local dishes in-cluding more exotic alligator and turtle offerings. If you're wary, don't be; nothing can taste bad when cooked in the spicy tomato gravy of a Cajun *sauce piquante*.

Continue till Louisiana 307 ends at Louisiana 20 (where a right turn joins Chapter 10). A left soon reaches **Chackbay** where ex-tremely popular Boudreaux's Restaurant inhabits an old service-sta-tion building. Boudreaux's menu is similar to Edwina's, typically Cajun with a hint of the exotic swamp. Sometimes dessert is the bayou spe-cialty, *tarte à la bouillie* (custard pie). If it's available order it! If not, plan a stop at Rouse's, a local supermarket with an in-house bakery, in Thibodaux or Raceland to pick up this treat. For the sweet-toothed, it's easily half the reason for making this trip.

Louisiana 20 turns into a fast-food four-lane entering **Thibodaux**, but this is Cajun country, so even the Howard Johnson hosts a rol-licking live-music Cajun dance every Saturday afternoon.

For Thibodaux's numerous downtown, northside, and westside plea-sures, cross the bayou (into Chapter 12). Otherwise turn left on Loui-siana 308 just before the bridge to follow Bayou Lafourche, the his-torical focus of all settlement, agriculture, trade, and daily life for a large slice of southeast Louisiana.

Rienzi Plantation (private) stands out with with its wrap-around galleries, matching curved stairways, and huge oaks. Seems fit for a queen? Rienzi was built in 1796 as never-used refuge for the Queen of Spain in case the French Revolution, and its guillotine, spread to her own country.

Across the bayou, Nicholls University's Ellender Library hosts the Center for Traditional Boatbuilding with displays of the unique local watercraft once so common on Bayou Lafourche. Bordering the college on the south, 1842 Acadia Plantation (private) sits on the spot where some say Jean Lafitte and Jim Bowie cooked up their infamous slave-smuggling racket in the 1810s.

Back on Louisiana 308, stop at Laurel Valley Plantation Store. Half gift shop, half museum, take time to wander through its narrow aisles crammed with a fun mix of souvenirs for sale and antiques on display. Outside, old farm equipment awaits inspection, including a "dummy," the narrow gauge locomotive that, before trucks, hauled cut sugar cane from wealthy planters' fields.

Now that you've had such a good time, get ready for the main attraction. Parish Road 33 leads from the bayou to seventy still-standing outbuildings. Workers' cabins, blacksmith and cooperage barns, schoolhouse and mill ruins make this one of the most complete plantation complexes anywhere in the South. The empty buildings provide an eerie reminder of the many people who called this village home, but the land around them remains a working plantation, so please stay off the private side roads.

Louisiana 308 passes under the Southern Pacific tracks at **Lafourche Crossing**. In 1852, when the railroad came through, the planter-aristocrats of Thibodaux made sure the new-fangled conveyance's noise, soot, and yellow fever contagion were kept well south of town. As at Des Allemands, the strategic crossroads of tracks and bayou made Lafourche Crossing a Civil War battlefield.

Back then, whiskey was a small but legitimate portion of troops' rations. When Rebels captured a Union wagonload of it in Thibodaux on June 20th, 1863, they spent a full twenty-four hours consuming the spoils of war. Thus fortified, they made three successive—and unsuccessful—cavalry charges over storm-muddied ground here before deciding the Yankees could keep Lafourche Crossing.

Continuing southeast, notice occasional remnants of a bayouside levee once as tall and extensive as the Mississippi's, but made redun-

Rienzi Plantation

dant when the entire bayou was dammed off from its source after an especially disastrous 1903 flood. Pasturage and cane fields are broken by houses, some old, some new, of plantations and *habitations* (small farms).

The story of the prairie Cajuns is told in Chapter 14, but the tale of Bayou Lafourche's Cajuns is perhaps even more touching. While some

Acadians braved open boats and overland treks to escape to Louisiana from their 1755 diaspora in Pennsylvania, Virginia, and the Carolinas, other exiles languished in internment camps in England. Later shipped to France, these New World pioneers became Old World misfits, never quite adjusting, subsisting on welfare till finally a Spanish settlement scheme offered passage to this very bayou. The woman in the bonnet you see hoeing her garden, the boy who waves to you from his fishing spot, the weathered gents you overhear speaking French in the grocery store—they're all descendants of the passengers of seven shiploads of Acadians who ended their exile here in 1785.

Approaching **Raceland**, two houses (both private) stand out. An 1890s Creole cottage, Khi Oaks takes its name from the grove that surrounds it. A mile farther down Louisiana 308, 1814 Rosella Plantation was built with the broad raised galleries of the Louisiana Colonial style.

Raceland was named for an 1850s horse track (the town's St. Mary's Catholic Church dates from that era) but was long overshadowed by the nearby cypress-mill town of Bowie. Bowie burned to the ground in 1917, and as adjacent swamps were largely lumbered out, it was never rebuilt.

Turn left on Louisiana 3199 and go through Raceland's faded downtown and past the century-old sugar mill where each fall sweet white smoke still pours from the chimneys. The fluffy conical hills off to the right are bagasse, the squeezed-out pulp of sugar cane, which is manufactured into wall board. Three miles farther, the road joins U.S. Route 90 again for the trip back to New Orleans.

Or, stay on Louisiana 308 till the next bridge crossing the bayou to Louisiana 1 and into the next chapter.

For more information:

Lafourche Tourist Commission 504-537-5800
    P.O. Box 340, Raceland, LA 70394
Torres Cajun Swamp Tours 504-633-7739

101 Torres Road, Highway 307, Thibodaux, LA 70301
Zam's Swamp Tours/Edwina's Restaurant 504-633-7881
  135 Kraemer Bayou Road, Thibodaux, LA 70301
Boudreaux's Restaurant 504-633-2382
  Route 20, Chackbay, LA 70301
Laurel Valley Village Plantation Museum.................... 504-446-7456
  Louisiana Highway 308, Thibodaux, LA 70301

CHAPTER 9

DOWN THE BAYOU

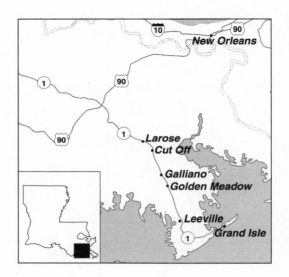

rom **NEW ORLEANS to GRAND ISLE**, via Bayou Lafourche through Lockport, Cut Off, and fishing villages. Features shrimp boats, seafood restaurants, unique shops, Mardi Gras rituals, fishing, and an island resort. A hundred and ten miles each way.

Louisiana is shaped like a worn-out boot with toes poking through the front. Each toe marks current or former paths of the fickle Mississippi River, and each offers an eventually dead-end road that makes a fascinating wetlands day trip from New Orleans.

Follow Louisiana 46 past Battle of New Orleans ramparts to Isleño country, haunt of Spanish-speaking Canary Islanders who settled here two centuries ago. Or follow Louisiana 23 down the west bank of the river skirting orange groves and Croatian oystering villages to historic Fort Jackson, and perhaps order a dozen on the half-shell at Miljak's Restaurant in **Empire**. Or follow Louisiana 45 for the national park and Filipino-Cajun shrimping village both named after pirate-turned-hero Jean Lafitte.

But our route goes down the next toe west, along Bayou Lafourche to where Louisiana 1 ends at the sea. Leave New Orleans on Interstate 10 west, and go to Interstate 310 south, and then to U.S. Route 90 west. Crossing Bayou Lafourche, curl onto the Louisiana 1 exit. The visitors center under the bridge offers a wealth of area info.

Even if you don't grab a free map, it's very hard to get lost. Louisiana 1 south hugs the west bank of the bayou—and sometimes even seems to overhang it—almost until both end at the Gulf of Mexico. The only other road of much consequence, Louisiana 308, hugs the east bank, usually in plain sight of Louisiana 1.

Colonial land grants fronting the bayou ran back from it forty arpents, about a mile and a half. When a landowner died, every heir wanted fertile bayou frontage, so the estate was split lengthwise. Next generation, same thing. Today, some tracts measure as little as twenty-six feet wide, but still a mile and a half deep! Houses so closely spaced, even in rural areas, earn Louisiana 1 the nickname, "the longest street."

For Cajuns living along it, north, south, east, and west are replaced by four more relevant directions: up, down, front, and back. Up means upstream; down, its opposite. Front means toward the bayou; back, away from it. When someone says, "I'll meet you in front, *cher*," you know to look for them at the bayouside. If they tell you, "I'm taking a walk in back," it means they're trudging away from the bayou to check their cattle, pick their pole beans, or maybe hunt blackberries in the woods.

If leaving the front implies fleeing its (by bayou standards) hectic pace, maybe that's why the farming community of **Vacherie-Gheens**, way in back along Louisiana 654, has managed to hold onto some very old carnival traditions. After a midday Mardi Gras parade, folks remain gathered along the roadside waiting.... Here they come: a troop of costumed young men—wielding whips! Well, actually switches, but everyone falls to their knees begging "Pardon! Pardon!" which usually earns a light tap. Insolence brings heavier blows and if anyone tries to escape, the chase is on! A relic of pre-Christian fertility rituals, the Gheens Mardi Gras welcomes tourists, but is not advised for the easily bruised.

South of Gheens on Louisiana 308 is lovely Clotilda Plantation, a 1900 raised cottage. On the west bank, Louisiana 1 curves back from the bayou to cross the Company Canal into **Lockport**. Originally called Longueville, and first settled before the Louisiana Purchase, Lockport blossomed after this 1847 canal made it a water-route crossroads. The old locks are now derelict, but a pretty park occupies the canal bank where mules plodded to tow schooners along *à la cordelle*, and Lockport is still enough of a water hub to make it a good place to buy a cooler full of crabs on your way back to the city. While you're at it, explore the bayouside's old downtown where a onetime bank is undergoing renovation as the Bayou Lafourche Folklife and Heritage Museum.

Bouverans, an 1862 Creole cottage a mile south of town, is a rare example of a plantation house built during the Civil War. A mile farther, across from a particularly grand 1920s bungalow, are overgrown remnants of the tall levee that once lined both banks the length of the bayou. Over time the levees were hauled away by the wheelbarrowful to build up soggy lawns. The sugar cane fields they once protected remain, now made safe by flood-control structures far upstream.

At enormous Bollinger Shipyard on the east bank, welders in face masks and colorful turned-back caps assemble everything from Coast Guard cutters to gambling riverboats. Most enterprises on the bayou are much smaller: a fisherman's boat moored in front of his home, a truck farmer's roadside vegetable stand. In **Larose**, from October to

December, Lafont's Citrus sells oranges, satsumas, and kumquats from their groves in the back, by the sack or as potted trees. Mr. Lafont also deals a little fresh honey, surplus of the bees that do his pollinating.

Again, Louisiana 1 peels back from the bayou to cross the busy Intracoastal Waterway, successor to Lockport's Company Canal. The villages from here to the Gulf owe their livelihood to the sea: to the shrimp, oysters, and fish in it and to the petroleum and natural gas under it. Fishing and work boats of every description crowd the bayou: tall-masted seagoing shrimp trawlers; high-prowed, flat-decked supply boats; low-slung, canopied luggers with elaborate railings to keep oysters on deck; flat-nosed push boats with fanglike bumpers; home-made skiffs of imaginatively varied shapes and levels of craftsmanship. Names in bold letters dress every bow: *Mr. Rusty, Laura P., Captain August, Tee Jo-Jo*.

Short dead-end streets (in Cajun called *manches*, sleeves) rib the highway. Typically, each is lined with the homes of one extended family, the result of property grown too narrow to divide lengthwise any longer.

Watch for Galjour's Bakery in Larose, but don't go in expecting a lot of fancy cookies and cakes. Galjour's specializes in crusty-outside, cottony-inside, flavorful French bread. There's also the saucer-sized, inch-thick crackers known as hardtack. Like centuries of sailors, bayou fishermen carry hardtack to sea—it keeps forever!

The local cuisine can be sampled at Franko's, where seafood gumbo competes on the menu with skinless fried-whole chicken and local favorite white beans and rice.

Cut Off, named after a long-disappeared short-cut canal, was the village where farmers spreading down the bayou bumped into fisherman retreating inland from the storm-battered coast. Two showpiece houses reflect those migrations. The east bank, up-the-bayou Ducos house was built on a manmade hill by prosperous sugar planters. The west bank, down-the-bayou Curole House, a double Creole cottage, was moved here in sections in 1893 after the coastal town it originally graced was destroyed by a hurricane.

Shrimp boats

Both of Cut Off's best-known tourist attractions are retail outlets, and both enjoy a national clientele through mail-order catalogs. The Cajun Pecan House is open October through Mardi Gras with pecan pies and pralines, Christmas fruit cakes, and Mardi Gras king cakes (a traditional sugared sweet-dough). At west 70th Street on the bayouside is the Louisiana Catalog Store, which we own. Begun in the late 1970s as a distributor for Glen's early movies, it's now a place to buy all that's fun and funky about Louisiana's cultural legacy. Trying not to tout it too shamelessly, the expansive store stocks beaucoup music, folk art, Native American crafts, goofy souvenirs, handmade jewelry, prints, puzzles, puppets, drygoods, foods and spices, and virtually every book in print about Louisiana.

Visitors to Cut Off (after they've spent their last dime at the Catalog Store) often like to stop at the Cut Off Net Shop past the church, where second and third generation net-makers will often chat with visitors, even as their fingers blur sewing shrimp nets for captains across the Gulf Coast. For lodging, Hassell House offers a woodsy, peaceful, "way in the back" bed and breakfast.

Cut Off blends into **Galliano** with neither sign nor seam. As the town's name might imply, not all bayou Cajuns are actually of Acadian descent. The fishermen who settled these towns included Italians, Irish, Germans, Filipinos, Houma Indians, and others who adopted the language of the dominant French-speaking culture.

Legend tells of a hurricane refugee whose home near the coast had been washed away. Coming up Bayou Lafourche on the rescue boat, he blinked his eyes in amazement when he saw his house, intact, perched on the bank where receding waters had left it. As the story goes, he swam to shore, moved back in, and thereby founded the town of **Golden Meadow**.

True or not, the town's name comes from an early 1900s marsh-drainage real-estate scheme thought up by northern industrialists. Cajuns call their town Canal d'Yankee. The golden meadows referred to fields of railroad daisies (*pisse-au-lit*), a flower Cajun lore says causes bed-wetting. However inauspicious such beginnings, the town boomed with the discovery of oil in 1938. For almost that long, Randolph's Restaurant on Louisiana 1 has been a local institution. Chef Randy

Cheramie recommends the seafood platter: "Shrimp, fish, oysters, stuffed crab, it makes you want to cry all that fresh seafood is so good!"

Golden Meadow sits on land that keeps trying to be water, so a short bayouside sea wall protects it against high tides. Drive slowly. The town earns its reputation as a speed trap. But also take time to pause near the Catholic Church, where a homemade but very elaborate shrine invites passers-by to a moment's reflection. Farther, a mounted heirloom shrimp boat, *Le Petit Caporal*, honors the local fishery. Religious and seafaring traditions come together with colorful pageantry each August at the Blessing of the Fleet, an annual event since 1916.

South of Golden Meadow, Houma Indians inhabit storm-battered houses and rusty mobile homes on the edge of a treeless landscape old maps referred to as "Trembling and Impassable Prairie." Houses give way to vast, wide-open marsh, too water-logged for man except the occasional fur trapper, but a great spot for birding.

At **Leeville** the road crosses then parts from Bayou Lafourche. Coastal erosion eats twenty-five square miles of Louisiana coastline every year, an acre every fifteen minutes. As incredible as those statistics are, they become easy to believe when you look out from the Leeville Bridge at the broken patches of salt marsh. Less than a century ago, this town was famous for plantations and orange groves. In front of Boudreaux Motel, a large-scale outdoor model re-creates the village as it looked before its destruction by hurricane in 1915. Leeville rose again with the 1930 discovery of oil and survives today as a staging area for offshore fields.

Bayou Moreau, once a settled waterway, has eroded into little more than Louisiana 1's roadside ditch. Long-dead but salt-pickled oak trees stand with branches twisted as if grimacing in pain. Enterprising Grand Isle merchants pepper Moreau with advertising signs, sometimes a dozen in a well-spaced row, each protruding from the water with a single word—"Fresh" "Bait" "Cold" "Beer"—a bit of ingenuity where the first hurricane would turn a normal billboard into a kite.

Does this flat horizon of marsh grass seem an odd spot to find a classy restaurant? Toupsie's combines the freshest Gulf seafood with imaginative recipes in a rather elegant atmosphere. Like most buildings this close to the coast, it perches high on stilts. Even at ground level, you can see for miles in this terrain, but being ten feet up provides a view of a pond-pocked prairie that stretches forever. For quicker stops, a lunch counter in the adjacent convenience mart offers poboys and shrimp burgers.

Port Fourchon caps side-road Louisiana 3090 with a collection of shrimp sheds and fuel docks bustling under the whir of helicopters coming and going offshore. Its public beach, notorious for dangerous riptides, looks across the Gulf to dozens of nearby offshore oil platforms—their lights flashing and horns beeping, peopled with roughnecks and roustabouts who work seven days on, seven days off. While perhaps not a setting of beauty, it's a world few landlubbers get to see.

After Fourchon, Louisiana 1 bends east toward **Cheniere Caminada**, where a wooden cross, a stone monument, and a few wind-bent oak trees mark a small cemetery. Caminadaville was once a thriving fishing port, the largest on the Louisiana coast. On October 1st, 1893, the Saturday dance ended early because of worsening weather. By morning, nearly half the town's citizens had drowned. Glen's grandfather, a boy of thirteen then, spent that night tied to the branch of an oak tree, but not quite high enough. When Glen himself was a boy, he'd hear the old man sob as he remembered the sea pulling at him—and washing from his arms a baby brother he'd never see again.

After burying what bodies could be found, survivors abandoned the town. With the arrival of the highway in the 1930s, people began to move back. Nowadays, Cheniere boasts a much-favored restaurant, Cigar's, where fishing boats literally dock against the kitchen to unload. But most houses you see are actually what south Louisianians call "camps."

Fishermen and trappers' thrown-together shacks continued to be called camps long after they developed permanency. Beach houses devoted to leisure are also called camps, even when quite civilized. Crossing the bridge onto **Grand Isle**, half the fun of driving Louisiana 1's final seven miles derives from reading the clever names bestowed on cherished getaways: Play Pen, Second Childhood, Bubba's Palace.

Grand Isle's glory days were in the 1890s, when New Orleans Creoles claimed it as their posh resort. Author Kate Chopin set her novel *The Awakening* here. Winding lanes among the oaks in the center of the island still taste of old Grand Isle, but the gracious hotels, bath houses, gambling halls, observatory, and mule-drawn tram were blown away by the same storm that devastated Cheniere Caminada. Today's vacationers stay at the clean-but-sometimes-weathered tourist courts dotting the beach front. Eateries, barrooms, tackle and souvenir shops abound.

Grand Isle State Park, near the far end of the island, is perfect for a day on the beach or overnight camping. Generally, the surf is gentle and the slope gradual enough for even toddlers to delight in the water or chase a *touloulou* (fiddler crab) as parents watch from the beach. These are not the pristine white sand beaches of Florida. On the other hand, bounty awaits any licensed fisherman who casts for speckled trout or runs a crab line. A long wooden pier offers fishing or the chance to watch Louisiana's largest colony of brown pelicans do their own kind of fishing.

From Bayou Rigaud on the northeast corner of the island, boats charter fishing trips to offshore "blue water." While myriad species of snapper, marlin, tuna, shark, and drum are plentiful, the traditional game fish of choice is *grand écaille* (tarpon). Grand Isle's annual Tarpon Rodeo, held each July since 1928, is one of the world's most famous and well-attended fishing tournaments.

At Grand Isle's very eastern tip, a Coast Guard station minds Barataria Pass, much as it was guarded in the mid-1800s by Fort Livingston, a crumbling but still-huge edifice visible across the channel. Before the fort was built, that island was home of Jean Lafitte, the privateer, smuggler, and pirate who, around 1810, launched what may have been America's first organized crime syndicate.

Lafitte flaunted his ill-gotten gains. When Louisiana's governor offered $500 for his capture, Lafitte offered $5000 for capture of the governor. A sun-battered Grand Isle fisherman told us the story of Francois Rigaud, a long-ago local planter, who one evening was playing cards with the boss of Barataria.

"The pot got so big, neither one would trust the other to cut the cards! What to do? So Rigaud rows home to Grand Isle, wakes up his five-year-old girl, tells his wife to keep quiet, and rows back across the pass... so his little daughter can cut the cards."

Lafitte won anyway. Staring across the water at the ruins and watching porpoises dance in the channel, we imagine the table piled with booty and listen for the creak of Francois Rigaud's oars.

For more information:

Lafourche Tourist Commission 504-537-5800
  P.O. Box 340, Raceland, LA 70394
Cajun Pecan House 504-632-2337
  14808 West Main, Cut Off, LA 70345
Louisiana Catalog Store 800-375-4100
  14839 West Main, Cut Off, LA 70345
Hassell House Bed and Breakfast 504-632-8088
  550 East 74th Street, Cut Off, LA 70345
Franko's Restaurant 504-798-7644
  13944 West Main, Larose, LA 70373
Randolph's Restaurant.. 504-475-5272
  806 South Bayou Drive, Golden Meadow, LA 70357
Toupsie's Restaurant 504-396-2727
  27900 Highway 1, Leeville, LA 70358
Cigar's Cajun Cuisine 504-787-2188
  Highway 1, Cheniere Caminada, LA 70358
Grand Isle State Park 504-787-2559
  P.O. Box 741, Grand Isle, LA 70358

CHAPTER 10

THE GREAT
RIVER ROAD

From **NEW ORLEANS to BATON ROUGE** along River Road, a hundred miles, with a thirty-mile side trip to the west bank at Vacherie. Features plantations, churches, country restaurants, African American history, and Christmas bonfires. Note: Houses mentioned are open for tours ($5-$10) unless indicated as private.

Driving west on Interstate 10, the road climbs to cross wetlands. Exit onto Interstate 310 over a dense cypress swamp toward Boutte (BOO-tee). Approaching the Mississippi, the land rises, which is one reason why plantations are along the river. Exit before the Hale Boggs/Luling Bridge onto Louisiana 48 and turn left.

Downriver is Destrehan Plantation. One of the oldest standing homes in the Mississippi Valley, it was built between 1787 and 1790 on the eve of great changes. As soon as Bienville selected the soggy site of New Orleans in 1718, entrepreneurs began procuring nearby waterfront lands. From West Africa, they imported seed and also slaves who possessed the technology to cultivate rice and process indigo into dye. In 1795, one entrepreneur, Etienne de Boré, perfected crystallization of local molasses into sugar. Sugar cane quickly became the king crop.

Remember two things as you tour, or simply ogle from the roadside, the River Road plantations. First, people then, like now, were fools for fashion who periodically remodeled their homes to the latest vogue. Thus, 1790 French-Caribbean Destrehan wears an 1830s renovation of big columns in the Greek Revival style brought west by Anglo American planters. Until the 1900s, River Road plantation houses were distinguished as Creole or Anglo by their exteriors, the former preferring color (and sometimes several of them), the latter, austere white.

Secondly, Destrehan's "big house," where the planter's extended family lived, is all that remains of its antebellum agro-industrial complex. Surrounding it were once an overseer's house, row upon row of slave quarters, livestock and sugar barns, blacksmith shop, mill, corn crib, carriage house, horse stable, *pigeonnier*, kitchen, laundry, milking shed, even a school and chapel. With the demise of plantation life, such outbuildings went unrepaired and eventually came down, leaving the big house to tell the plantation's story.

Upriver, 1790 Ormond Plantation Bed and Breakfast exhibits antique dolls, guns, and slot machines. Like numerous homes, its builder was African American. Many of Louisiana's free people of color were respected architects, furniture makers, painters, masons, and the metal workers who created New Orleans's famous wrought-iron balconies.

But for most Blacks, life then meant unending field work. In 1811, this stretch of river saw one of America's largest slave revolts. Hundreds formed an army and marched on New Orleans, only to be defeated by a better-equipped militia in a bloody, one-sided battle. More often, desperate slaves would simply run away, taking refuge with Indians or colonies of fellow maroons in the swamp.

Between Destrehan and Ormond is St. Charles Borromeo Church, the 1921 replacement for the "Little Red Church" founded by German colonists in the earliest days of the colony. Germans and Swiss were lured to this "German Coast" with promise-them-anything advertising. Irate at being so duped and repeatedly refused permission to return to Europe, they eventually made the best of the "howling wilderness." By 1724, their gardens and livestock kept New Orleans from starvation.

"We're still here," affirms a descendant. "It's just the German names got turned into French: Foltz is Folse, Trischl is Triche, Wagensbach is Waguespack…"

It was upon sighting the Little Red Church that steamboat crews, by tradition, would demand their wages before completing the downriver trek into New Orleans. Nowadays, seamen from ocean ships dock at the plants, refineries, and grain elevators edging the river. It's not uncommon to see Greek or Filipino sailors hiking over the levee to a River Road saloon.

Louisiana 628 traverses Bonnet Carre, site of an 1874 crevasse (levee break) and now a relief spillway when spring high water in the Mississippi threatens New Orleans. From its levee crossings, you can see the containment dome of Waterford nuclear plant on the far bank, as well as ships and barges plying the river. Bulk carriers steam upstream sitting high in the water, but put back to sea heavy with grain or coal. Tankers importing foreign oil do just the opposite, traveling upriver full and downriver empty. Barges that haul Iowa corn and Minnesota wheat trade for Louisiana salt to melt winter snow off those states' roads.

In **LaPlace** where Louisiana 28 turns into Louisiana 44, follow Main Street away from the river to Airline Highway (U.S. Route 61). This precursor to Interstate 10 was built by Governor Huey Long to connect Louisiana's governmental capital to its commercial one.

For us, it connects to Airline Motors Restaurant, the neon king of roadside diners, a short jump right. It looks like a 1939 Art Deco auto dealership because it was. Now it's the perfect, round-the-clock spot for a cup of joe, a slice of pie, or a meal. Waitresses are friendly, restrooms sparkle, and counter service (love those spinning stools) is brisk.

Back on Louisiana 44, continue upriver. At **Reserve**, past the ferry landing, the 1760 Godchaux Plantation is undergoing restoration. The old Godchaux Sugar complex, grain elevators, and refineries line the road to San Francisco Plantation, the bright gingerbread house that first inspired the description "steamboat gothic." The interiors are even showier, fully restored to an elaborate 1860s decor of ceiling frescoes, colorful textiles, and a generally flagrant display of what money could buy before the Civil War. With many plantations so starkly restored, a tour of San Francisco is a refreshing reminder of what show-offs antebellum planters often were.

A mile farther, Louisiana 54 leads back to the old cypress logging company town of **Garyville**, with its Timbermill Museum in the turn-of-the-century Lyon Lumber Company building. Besides models, photos, and artifacts, a visit includes a peek inside the document-crammed room-sized company safe.

The town of **Gramercy**, once called Cabanocey ("where ducks roost"), is on a stretch of river named "the Acadian Coast" after its French-speaking settlers. Adjacent **Lutcher** came later, born of the cypress-lumbering boom. Mill workers' cottages still line Texas and Cypress Streets in old downtown north of the tracks.

Long famous for a now-dwindling crop of aromatic Perique tobacco (a few drying barns remain off Louisiana 642 upriver), today this area is much better known for another source of combustion. Every fall, families and clubs build twenty-foot-high bonfires, sometimes modeled into locomotives, ferry boats, or plantations. Stretching along the levee for miles, in century-old tradition, the Bonfires on the Levee are set ablaze on Christmas Eve to help guide Papa Noel on his appointed rounds.

From here, we recommend an optional but fascinating side trip to the west bank and some of the river's best-loved plantations. Cross the Veterans Memorial River Bridge at Gramercy. On Louisiana 18, the west bank's River Road, head upriver toward **Vacherie**, a Bayou Goula Indian village and later cattle-ranching area, where fascinating Laura Plantation is located.

A unique Creole complex, Laura's remarkable twelve buildings include two manor houses and the slave quarters where, in the 1870s, the West African folk tales of Br'er Rabbit were first recorded in America. The architectural contributions of Senegalese artisans are also featured, but Laura's moving history is brought to life most through the memoirs of its namesake mistress. The survival of her diaries paints a much fuller picture of plantation life than the scattered family legends that suffice on most plantation tours.

Continuing upriver, pause for a look at 1851 Felicity and 1820 St. Joseph before Oak Alley comes into view. Among the most photographed of houses anywhere, Oak Alley is renowned for its double row of tremendous oaks which pre-date the house. Overnight cottages and a restaurant make it a popular weekend getaway spot.

Downriver from the bridge, Whitney Plantation (private), set in a copse of trees, begs for restoration. Legend says this 1803 raised cottage's interior frescoes were the thanks of an artist who fell sick painting a nearby church and was nursed by Whitney's mistress. Two miles farther, Evergreen (private) dominates the roadside with its magnificent, curved stairway. This 1840s Greek Revival's rare extensive outbuildings include a kitchen, guest house, *garçonnières*, stables, slave cabins, privies, and an overseer's home.

Crossing back to the east bank, a necklace of Creole cottages lines Louisiana 44 into **Convent**. They hardly prepare you for massive Manresa. Three stories high and twenty-two columns wide, it was built in 1831 as Jefferson College, a private school for planters' sons. During the Civil War, federal troops had their barracks here, and afterwards, the owner gave it to the Catholic Church. Since 1931, it's served as a laymen's retreat.

Not nearly as big, but equally grand, St. Michael's Church features

San Francisco Plantation House

an 1856 pipe organ and a gloriously ornate hand-carved altar originally displayed at the 1889 Paris World's Fair. Behind it hides an
1876 Lourdes Grotto for special devotions. In the adjacent cemetery, graves much older than the church reflect the gumbo of peoples
who tilled these lands: Acadians, Germans, French Colonials. We
were surprised to find the archaic Old French *Ci Git* (Here Lies)
marking many graves and astounded by a crypt, as big as a cottage,
made entirely of cast iron!

We might have stayed longer, but we were growing hungry. Perfect
timing! On River Road just south of the Sunshine Bridge, forty-year-
old Hymel's (EE-mells) Restaurant is an off-the-beaten-path treasure.
A big, unpretentious dining room with an attached saloon, Hymel's
is known for seafood and reasonable prices. The tasty turtle soup reduced us to grunts and sighs.

Re-energized, we zipped up River Road to Tezcuco Plantation. The
name of this 1855 Greek Revival raised cottage means resting place in
Aztec; its original owner was a Mexican War veteran. Current owners
have Tezcuco living up to its name. A row of charming cottages makes
a bed-and-breakfast village complimented by a restaurant, antique shop,
and most interesting of all, the African American Museum and Gallery. Though compact, its displays fill a big gap in telling the story of
the plantation quarters, so different from life in the big house.

Just up the road, Louisiana 44 splits from River Road to become
Louisiana 75, the proverbial fork in the road. Following Louisiana 44
leads to the Cabin Restaurant, a cute collection of restored houses
and stores, exceedingly popular with tour groups.

The Cajun Village, on Louisiana 22, is another charming assemblage of old buildings filled with gift shops, tourist info, a coffee house,
and the fantastic Southern Tangent Gallery. This last is packed with
original works by local artists: intricate voodoo dolls, hand-carved
wood paintings, even giant herons made of driftwood.

Interstate 10 and Baton Rouge are minutes away if you can steel
yourself past the fifty-six-store Tanger Outlet Mall along the way. Or
take Louisiana 70 to the Sunshine Bridge and across to Chef John
Folse's high-end-but-worth-every-penny (and calorie) Lafitte's Land-

ing Restaurant, a few miles to Bayou Lafourche and Chapter 12.

Our chosen option was to continue along River Road's (Louisiana 75) many wonders. A mile past the Louisiana 44 turn-off, Houmas House has extensive antique furnishings. The next two grand, private homes along River Road were wedding presents from planter Marius Bringier to his daughter and son, 1801 Bocage and 1821 L'Hermitage.

Captivating Ashland-Belle Helene may look familiar due to its use in several Hollywood movies. The classically beautiful house is a true example of Greek Revival: from a distance, it genuinely looks like an ancient temple. Though repainted and spruced up by its new owner, the Shell Chemical Company, it's now closed to the public.

It's the great irony of River Road that these glorious monuments to the past are often neighbored by odoriferous refineries, but plantation-sized tracts of land adjacent to the ocean ship-navigable river proved irresistible to industry.

Carville, hometown of James Carville, the "Ragin' Cajun" who ran Bill Clinton's 1992 presidential campaign, is also home to Indian Camp Plantation. Built in 1847 on the site of a Houma Indian village, it's now the only remaining leprosarium in the United States. Opened in 1896, this sprawling complex housed hundreds of patients. A cure having been found, it's now home to a handful. Hansen's Disease is not the contagious scourge of Biblical lore. Weekday tours are offered.

Commuting hours only, a ferry crosses from the Hansen's Center to **White Castle** and Nottaway. Or backtrack to Louisiana 75 and the St. Gabriel Catholic Church. Undergoing restoration, this simple frame structure was built in 1769 and may be a replica of the church Acadians attended before their 1755 exile from Nova Scotia.

From St. Gabriel, Louisiana 75 continues past the hundred-year-old Barthell's Grocery and the considerably more modern Ciba Chemical Plant (tours by appointment) to the Plaquemine ferry. Otherwise, Louisiana 74 leads to Interstate 10 and Baton Rouge.

Of the capital's many attractions, one for country-road lovers stands out. At the Essen Lane exit off Interstate 10, the Louisiana State University Rural Life Museum features a mesmerizing accumulation of artifacts ranging from prehistory to grandpappy's day. AND a plantation complex of many authentic, moved-to-this-site buildings, such as slave quarters, commissary, mill, and barns. AND a half dozen other buildings each representing a traditional Louisiana house type, such as a shotgun house, Acadian cottage, and dogtrot cabin.

This is definitely not Colonial Williamsburg—the staff is low-key and so is the admission fee. There's so much to dawdle over and so many places to poke your nose, it's easy to spend a half day or more. We've done it lots of times. As a matter of fact, tomorrow...

For more information:

Destrehan Plantation 504-764-9315
    13034 River Road, P.O. Box 5, Destrehan, LA 70047
Ormond Plantation Bed and Breakfast 504-764-8544
    13786 River Road, Destrehan, LA 70047
St. Charles Parish Tourist Info 504-783-5140
    P.O. Box 302, Hahnville, LA 70057
San Francisco Plantation 504-535-2341
    P.O. Box AX, Highway 44, Reserve, LA 70084
Garyville Timbermill Museum 504-535-3202
    P.O. Box 867, Garyville, LA 70051
St. James Parish/Gramercy-Lutcher Tourism 504-869-9752
    P.O. Box 426, Gramercy, LA 70052
Laura Plantation 504-265-7690
    2247 Highway 18, Vacherie, LA 80090
Oak Alley Plantation Bed and Breakfast 504-265-2151
    3645 Highway 18, Vacherie, LA 70090
Ascension Parish Tourist Info 504-675-6550
    6470 Highway 22, Suite A, Sorrento, LA 70778
Tezcuco Plantation Bed and Breakfast 504-562-3929

3138 Highway 44, Darrow, LA 70725

Houmas House 504-473-7841
   40136 Highway 942, Darrow, LA 70725-2302

Hansen's Disease Center/Carville 504-642-4736
   Carville, LA 70721

Iberville Parish/St. Gabriel Tourism 800-233-3560
   P.O. Box 248, Plaquemine, LA 70765

Ciba Tours 504-642-1286
   P.O. Box 11, St. Gabriel, LA 70776

LSU Rural Life Museum 504-765-2437
   4600 Essen Lane, Baton Rouge, LA 70898

Baton Rouge Visitors Bureau 800-LA-ROUGE
   P.O. Box 4149, Baton Rouge, LA 70821

CHAPTER 11
THE FELICIANAS

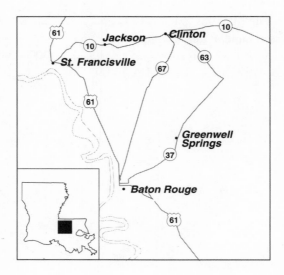

rom **BATON ROUGE** and back, ninety-two miles via Clinton, Jackson, and St. Francisville. Features antebellum plantations and towns, wineries, historic cemeteries, and the Tunica hills.

Greenwell Springs Road (Louisiana 37) is one of several east-west Baton Rouge thoroughfares always under construction yet never quite wide enough to handle rush-hour traffic. Persevere, fellow traveler. By the time you actually reach the village of **Greenwell Springs**, pleasant semirural suburbs give way to tree-draped roads through se-

rene country hills. In fall, the olive- and orange-leafed wood lots parade into bright rye-grass horse pastures. Proceeding north, across the
Comite River, pines grow thicker, or cut over, in patches of managed
forest.

Louisiana 37 leads to **Greensburg**, itself quite historic, but instead veer left onto Louisiana 63 just before the Amite River. Our
goal is the Felicianas, that fabled region of rolling hills and grand
upland plantations named by Spanish Governor Bernardo de Galvez
for his beloved wife, Felice. Ah! How could this help but be a roman-
tic journey?

After thirteen undulating miles northwest, Louisiana 63 dead-ends
into Louisiana 67 on the edge of **Clinton**. A right turn leads to
LeBlanc's Restaurant, for breakfast or buffet lunch, where forks clat-
ter against servers queries "Whats'ya two vegetables? Whats'ya starch?"
Ahead are the half-hidden Doric columns of the Greek Revival Brame-
Bennett House bed and breakfast.

A friend recently asked, "Why visit cemeteries, when someday you'll
be spending all your time in one?" If you share that sentiment, skip
this next bit of tour. But if, like us, you cherish an eloquent epitaph as
a window to another time, then at the Louisiana 10 crossroads turn
right. Past gracious town homes is the Masonic Cemetery. Along its
western fence, tall headstones and pillars define a Jewish section much
larger than expected for a small, Protestant town. Poignant inscrip-
tions memorialize youths taken in their prime or old folks born in
1800s Bavaria and Alsace who died three-quarters of a century later
and thousands of miles away. One stone tells of a young man who
"loved his mother so much he prayed for her daily, even on his death-
bed." Another laments, "One by one life takes our treasures, all's left
of our own is our dead."

Continuing east is a much cheerier spot, Casa de Sue Winery. This
first of two wineries on this route is the smaller and by far the more
out-of-the-way. But its intimate family operation where Dad lugs cases
and Son gives genuinely interesting tours (sporting his high-school

letter jacket) is enjoyable enough to warrant the twenty-mile round trip. From Clinton, take Louisiana 10 east through five miles of rolling vistas, then right for another five on shaded, deep cut Gilead Road.

"Casa de Sue" is a play on the owner's Basque family name, Cazedessus. Such gentle humor flows as easily as the wine in the gift shop where matriarch Joanne conducts tastings of dry to semisweet vintages made from organically grown muscadine grapes and blueberries.

Back in Clinton, Louisiana 10 west fronts a square surrounding the monumental, still-in-daily-use 1840 Greek Revival courthouse. A billboard-sized map across the street charts a driving and/or walking tour of the town's historic buildings. Most famous is a whole block of single-story antebellum offices known as "Lawyers' Row." One is home to the Audubon Regional Library where you can peek in to admire the original plank floors and old mantels. South from the square on Bank Street, venerable Silliman College is the center of Clinton's April Arts & Crafts Festival, complete with buggy rides, garden tours, and antique sales.

Off Bank Street as well, Louisiana 10 continues east toward **Jackson**, crossing the bottoms of Pretty Creek and the Comite River before breaking into open pasturage interrupted by rambling, red-roofed Mission Revival buildings. These state-hospital colonies stretching from here into Jackson house the ill, the infirm, and the criminally insane.

In 1845, Benjamin Norman wrote of this area, "Here are some of the wealthiest and most intelligent planters, and the finest plantations in the state, the region of princely taste and luxury, and more than patriarchal hospitality." Many of those princely estates still stand today, some open for tours and as bed and breakfasts.

South of the Louisiana 68 crossroads is the 1830s Greek Revival Asphodel Plantation. As a restaurant and inn, it's long been an area favorite. To the north is the 1903 Queen Anne Glencoe Plantation (private). Victorian architecture enthusiasts must make this pilgrimage, even for naught but a roadside gander. Glencoe is huge, and very

Rosedown Plantation

one-of-a-kind with five different styles of fish-scale shingles and a mesmerizing roof line.

In these Feliciana Parish highlands, early wealth came from cotton which grew extraordinarily well in its loess, a wind-deposited topsoil as rich as the flood-deposited alluvial soils along the Mississippi and bayous, but minus the enormous expense of levee building those lowlands demanded. Though gorgeous plantation homes are found throughout the state, there is perhaps no greater concentration of them than in this region.

On the outskirts of Jackson is Feliciana Cellars. This winery bottles three distinctive muscadine wines and houses Rickenjack's popular lager and ale micro-brewery in its spacious hacienda-style building. A viewing gallery overlooks the tanks and vats and press operations, but we frankly preferred the tasting area where manager Jim Hendrickson plied us with samples and tales of leading the charge against the state's half-century-old prohibition laws. Even for teetotalers, this is a good stop for picking up Jackson's self-guided tour brochure.

Originally called Bear Corners (for the official state mammal whose range has since been reduced), the town was renamed for Andrew Jackson, hero of New Orleans. Perhaps such patriotism seemed prudent in an area partly settled by British loyalists fleeing the American Revolution. Most such Tories moved on or mended their ways. With the establishment of the state insane asylum here in 1847 (whose earliest buildings stand just past the winery), the town claimed a different sort of infamy as generations of children statewide taunted each other with being "sent to Jackson."

At bustling Charter Street Market, a giant parking-lot mural of the historic district will reorient you after a morning of tippling wine. Across the street, aromas waft from much-lauded Major's Bear Corners Restaurant. On the west side of town at Bobby's Drive Inn, box dinners and malteds harken back to teeny-bop years. It was all we could do to keep from necking in the car.

Jackson is crammed with historic structures. Charter Street's 1815 onion-domed bank, now the town hall, is our favorite. East College

Street's "Silk Stocking Avenue" is lined with vintage buildings and the truly exceptional West Florida Museum and Old Hickory Village. One of the state's most outstanding local museums, it invites a romp through time with everything from a 1920s theater organ to long-obsolete farm machinery. Just up the road, Centenary College Commemorative Area recalls Jackson's early educational institutions from 1826 on with an interpretive museum lodged in the campus's antebellum buildings.

West of Jackson, after three bridges in quick succession cross various branches of Thompson Creek, take a left onto Louisiana 965. Beyond the manicured greens of The Bluffs golf resort and restaurant and the wild woods of the Mary Ann Brown Nature Conservancy Preserve is the Audubon Commemorative Area. One hundred acres of nature trails surround the 1799 West Indies-style Oakley Plantation where John James Audubon started his famous *Birds of America*. Hired as tutor to the planter's daughter, Audubon was later booted out for alleged advances toward the young innocent.

From Oakley, should the day or your spirits be waning, Louisiana 965 continues to U.S. Route 61, the quickest way back to Baton Rouge. But we doubled back to Louisiana 10, then southwest toward St. Francisville. Another state commemorative area off Louisiana 10, tiny Locust Grove Cemetery is the resting place of Sarah Knox Taylor Davis, daughter of U.S. President Zachary Taylor and first wife of Confederate President Jefferson Davis. Nearby is General Eleazor Ripley, War of 1812 hero, and beside him, the petite grave of his infant daughter. Birds chirped overhead from fragrant sweet olive trees as we read her epitaph, "Stranger, if e'er these lines be read, mourn for the living not the dead."

Whew! Feeling suddenly very appreciative of each other, we drove on.

Nearing **St. Francisville**, the graceful entrance to Rosedown Plantation and Gardens announces its enormous canopied oak alley, extensive formal gardens of camellias, roses and azaleas woven with pathways and statuary, and unique outbuildings. Fine art, antiques, and

Bull riding / Angola Prison Rodeo

interiors include Henry Clay's unused presidential bedroom suite for which an additional wing was built.

Crossing U.S. Route 61 (Great River Road) into St. Francisville, take a left at the deadend, past rows of shanties. At Ferdinand Street is the Victorian Gothic St. Francisville Inn (also called the Wolf-Schlesinger House), a reasonable and very attractive bed and breakfast. A hop left is the cute Magnolia Cafe, but for the moment turn right with Louisiana 10 onto Ferdinand Street. Here, beautiful St. Francisville welcomes tourists with open arms. Among the cluster of enticing shops, an old hardware store shelters the West Feliciana Museum and Tourist Bureau. Amid old photographs, eighteenth-century utensils, and dioramas are detailed maps, brochures, and books of the historic district and area plantations. Even when it's closed, brochures are dispensed from a box on the porch.

For two and a half months in 1810, St. Francisville was the capital of an independent nation, the Republic of West Florida. Anglo planters had immigrated west from the United States into this French, then Spanish, then British, then once again Spanish colony upriver from New Orleans. As their numbers grew, their patience shrunk. Finally, they rose up and stormed the Spanish fort at Baton Rouge, proudly hoisted the Lone Star flag of their new country, then annexed themselves to the United States as fast as bureaucracy would allow. (Some thirty years later, the same scenario would be re-enacted on a much grander scale in Texas, Lone Star flag and all.)

Royal Street loops through St. Francisville's architectural feast of homes back to Our Lady of Mt. Carmel Catholic Church. Its designer, Louisiana native and West Point-trained engineer Pierre Beauregard, is better known for having commanded the attack on Fort Sumter which started the Civil War. The 1903 Beaux Arts courthouse faces Grace Episcopal, Louisiana's largest and best-preserved antebellum Gothic Revival church. In its cemetery, dense sweet olives shade the exquisite wrought-iron fences around handsome family tombstones. Sasanquas and camellias crowd founding mothers' and fathers' graves, a heartfelt reminder of the Felicianas's Anglo influence.

On the Mississippi's bank lies Bayou Sara. Arriving on New Year's

Day 1821, Audubon wrote, "We found two brigs at anchor, several steamers, and a number of flatboats, this being a place of considerable mercantile importance." Repeatedly ravaged by flood, little remains of Bayou Sara except the ferry landing for crossing the Mississippi to New Roads (and into Chapter 1).

North of St. Francisville on U.S. Route 61 are many fine houses. The Myrtles is known for its long verandas, exterior ironwork, interior plasterwork, and of course its ghosts. Butler-Greenwood has an elaborate Victorian parlor as well as the original kitchen and cook's cottage outbuildings. Afton Villa's big house burned in 1963, but its avenue of oaks still leads to a rare surviving example of plantation formal gardens (open spring only), and an explosion of color. Catalpa, an 1885 Victorian raised cottage is full of family antiques. The Cottage is one of the state's oldest plantation complexes with kitchen, school, milk house, barn, and slave cabin still on the property. There are plenty others, but you get the idea.

Turning west from U.S. Route 61 north onto Louisiana 66 (Angola Road) takes you toward Green Springs, Greenwood, Weyanoke, and Live Oak Plantations, and through the Tunica Hills, some of Louisiana's most ruggedly beautiful terrain.

If it's October, a Sunday, and adventure calls, save your afternoon for the Angola Prison Rodeo, an annual tradition for over a quarter of a century. Get there early to peruse the crafts prisoners hawk just inside the walls. The Wild West action traditionally starts around 2:00 P.M. as maximum security inmates try to out-macho each other riding broncos and roping bulls. As a friend says, "It's like watching the gladiators in *Spartacus*."

South of St. Francisville, U.S. Route 61 spins into **Baton Rouge**. On the way, Port Hudson Civil War Battlefield is a history-lover's paradise. A museum, outdoor displays, observation towers, and hiking trails over the six-hundred-and-forty-acre park explain the forty-eight-day campaign against "Fort Desperate," the longest siege in American military history. It was on this very battlefield that African American troops were first sent into the horrifying cauldron of combat.

For more information:

Brame-Bennett Plantation Bed and Breakfast 504-683-5241
227 South Baton Rouge Street, Clinton, LA 70722

Casa de Sue Winery.. 800-683-5937
14316 Hatcher Road, Clinton, LA 70722

City of Clinton 504-683-5145
P.O. Box 595, Clinton, LA 70722

Asphodel Plantation Bed and Breakfast 504-654-6868
Route 2, Box 89, Jackson, LA 70748

East Feliciana Parish/Jackson Tourist Commission 504-634-7155
P.O. Box 667, Jackson, LA 70748

Feliciana Cellars Winery 504-634-7982
1848 Charter Street, Jackson, LA 70848

West Feliciana/St. Francisville Tourist Info 504-635-6330
P.O. Box 1548, St. Francisville, LA 70775

Angola State Penitentiary (rodeo info) 504-655-4411
Angola, LA 70712

Port Hudson State Commemorative Area 504-654-3775
756 West Plains-Port Hudson Road, Zachary, LA 70791

CHAPTER 12

SAINTS AND
SUGAR CANE

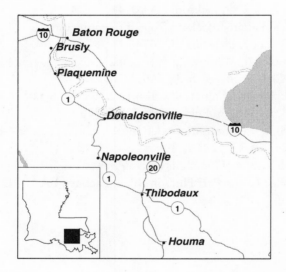

From **BATON ROUGE to HOUMA** along the west bank of the Mississippi and Bayou Lafourche. Ninety-five miles via Plaquemine, Donaldsonville, and Thibodaux. Features navigation locks, historic towns, beautiful churches, and grand sugar-cane plantations.

Our destination lies southeast, yet we start off due west, crossing the Mississippi River Bridge from Baton Rouge on Interstate 10 west. Such are the vagaries of geography along the sinuous Mississippi. Before clearing the bridge, follow the exit to Plaquemine.

If you enjoy boat watching or huge public works, track the "Port of Baton Rouge" signs to the Port Allen Locks. Venturing beyond the gates, curve upward to the main office parking area, then stroll toward the toots and honks. From a catwalk edging over the locks, you can watch push boats nudge enormous tows of barges into the steep-walled passageway, barely tucking them all in. This busy structure links the Mississippi to the Intracoastal Waterway and with it, Louisiana's vast web of bayous and canals.

South of the locks, leave four-lane Louisiana 1 with a left onto Louisiana 988. It turns into River Road as it loops past levee-grazing livestock, forgotten boroughs, and age-old plantations. In **Brusly**, workers from the 1871 Cinclaire Sugar Mill still fill the pews of the 1907 white frame St. John the Baptist Church; the three bells that call them to mass are named Jean, Marie, and Joseph. But 1830s graves in the adjacent cemetery remember an older chapel and a time when each plantation cooked cane juice in open kettles. Jumping from the past to the future, the humongous Dow Chemical plant (tours by appointment) produces ingredients for everything from medical plastics to salad dressing. Just past it, River Road snakes into **Plaquemine** through a knot of narrow streets known as Old Turnerville, where quaint 1800s homes are enjoying extensive restoration. Marietta's and Miss Louise's, facing each other across Nadler Street, offer tours and bed and breakfast.

Keep turning Old Turnerville's corners and eventually Louisiana 1 appears. Straight across the Bayou Plaquemine bridge is the City Cafe, a chummy lunch and supper favorite for almost eighty years whose blue-plate specials feature spaghetti and chicken-fried steak.

To view Plaquemine's restored nineteenth-century splendor, curl south with Louisiana 1. At LaBauve Street, go left for a block at the eye-popping Kearney Home, an early 1900s wedding gift. Come back up Church Street to Main where grandly Romanesque St. John the Evangelist boasts an ornate interior altar and some remarkable stained glass. In the next block stretch the columns of the 1849 courthouse.

Brochures, including a more detailed driving/walking tour, are available at the Plaquemine Lock Museum. Bayou Plaquemine had always been a spring-high-water short cut between the Mississippi and Atchafalaya Rivers. The lock, completed in 1909 (by an engineer who went on to design the Panama Canal locks), made it a year-round waterway until replaced in 1961 by the larger Port Allen lock upstream. An observation tower on the levee's edge climbs a heart-pumping forty feet. With lucky timing, we raced up its steps to the melody of a distant calliope. Our reward was a panoramic river view embellished by a paddle wheeler churning the brown Mississippi.

Heading out Eden Street (Louisiana 1 south), take a left onto Louisiana 75 to reach the river again. Here, a ferry crosses the Mississippi (into Chapter 11), but a right follows the levee downstream. Back when no word struck more fear than "Crevasse!" it was the responsibility of each planter to maintain the levee across his land and patrol it during high water. Now, the job is performed by the government and big machines. Not to worry, but it's a little-known fact that the levee you're following is a foot lower than the east bank's; in a worst-case flood, this side of the river will be sacrificed to save New Orleans.

Seven and a half miles below lovely St. Louis Plantation (private) is the 1902 Madonna Chapel (reconstructed in 1924). Take the key from the box by the door to let yourself into what bills itself as the world's smallest church. Light a candle to bless your prayers. More than likely you'll find candles glimmering from previous travelers.

Standing out from crumbling old farmhouses, Tallyho Plantation (private) is actually an overseer's house the family moved into when the big house burned. To see a truly jaw-dropping huge mansion, continue downriver to Nottaway.

Designed with both Greek Revival and Italianate features by renowned architect Henry Howard, Nottaway's fifty-three-thousand-square feet and fifty-plus rooms make it possibly the largest home in the South. Innovative indoor plumbing and gas lighting rendered it even more extraordinary when finished in 1859. What you may find most impressive today are its ironwork balconies and grand white ballroom. Sustaining itself on a brisk tourist trade, Nottaway has a restaurant and also welcomes overnight guests.

The River Road rejoins Louisiana 1 in **White Castle**, a turn-of-the-century lumber town named after a long-disappeared plantation even larger than Nottaway. How come the one that got away is always the bigger fish? White Castle offers Maggio's Antiques, one of our frequent stops, an interesting old downtown, and the White Castle Inn.

Angle back to River Road (Louisiana 405) to traipse past long, skinny shotgun houses and Creole cottages with their wide porches and two—occasionally even three or four—front doors. These are the architectural legacy of the West Indies. Multiple front doors channel breezes, and a *galerie*, or porch, provides cooling shade.

But many houses are empty, and many others rotted from neglect. Antebellum times saw multitudes living and working here, but tractors have replaced men and mule teams. Sugar-cane harvesters—you might see one cruising down the road, looking like a huge mechanical praying mantis—replaced the regiments of field hands who swung their long knives to cut the rows of green stalks.

How many ghosts must haunt these fields? How many haunt the row of "quarters," long without paint or repair, just past Mulberry Grove Plantation? Or the beguiling old brick schoolhouse falling to ruin on Noel Plantation? An intact marble cornerstone tells how this academy for plantation children was built in memoriam to the planter's own daughter, stolen so young by death.

The River Road coils back to Louisiana 1 at the Evan Hall Sugar Mill. Turn left to follow the Union Pacific tracks. Where Louisiana 1 takes a ninety-degree right turn, don't. Instead, continue straight on Louisiana 3089, crossing the bayou into **Donaldsonville**.

The bayou is Lafourche, "the fork," once called La Fourche des Chétimachas for a native tribe forced south into the swamps after they martyred a French missionary. Lafourche forks from the Mississippi to flow a hundred and twenty miles to the sea. Indeed it was actually the Mississippi until the river shifted two millennia ago.

Guarding this route, Donaldsonville was a gateway for settlers: Spanish-speaking soldier/farmers recruited in the Canary Islands, then French-speaking refugee Acadians, then English-speaking Virginia and Mississippi planters looking to cash in on the sugar boom. Out of the bayou flowed planters' molasses and contraband. The smuggler Jean Lafitte sent boats up Lafourche to bypass the customs house at New Orleans. Some say his entrepôt was Old Viala Plantation, now Chef John Folse's ritzy and deservedly famous Lafitte's Landing Restaurant, east of town at the foot of the Sunshine Bridge.

Turn left onto Railroad Avenue. Most of downtown dates from after the Civil War, when on August 9th, 1862, federal gunboats systematically shelled its buildings to rubble in reprisal for Confederate guerrillas sniping at them from the levee. To finish the job, "a detachment of Yankees went to shore with fire torches in hand," a Donaldsonville Creole remembered in her diary.

After the war, Italians came to dominate the mercantile district. Their influence lingers in the cuisine of Ruggiero's Restaurant and Dimm's Bakery, where horseshoe bread is yet a brisk seller. Another fun stop is Rossie's Ben Franklin, a classic five and dime that displays some very old wares as a sort of informal museum.

The Romanesque courthouse lies across Louisiana Square Park, its century-old detached jail now the Ascension Heritage Museum. At Railroad Avenue and the river front, the phenomenal 1878 Italianate Lemann Brothers department store, though now closed, still deserves a stroll under its loftily covered sidewalks. Beside its arched windows and cast-iron pilasters, you hardly need close your eyes to hear the clatter of hooves, the rustle of petticoats, the clack of a walking stick.

Turn right onto Mississippi Avenue to Ascension Catholic Church, a monumental 1875 Gothic edifice. From it, St. Vincent Street wanders through the old residential district of Iberville and Lessard Streets, where grand homes eventually give way to Victorian shotgun houses, one room wide and several deep.

Donaldsonville has a couple of memorable cemeteries. A few blocks behind the church, at the corner of St. Vincent and Claiborne, crypts rival in size and surpass in ornamentation the row houses a few blocks over. Most famous is the 1845 Egyptian-style Landry tomb designed by celebrated architect James Dakin, but it has many challengers. Our favorite was a Victorian Gothic priests' crypt of intricately carved white

E. D. White House

marble. But most touching was a child's tomb with this epitaph:

> There was an angel band in Heaven,
> That was not quite complete,
> So God took our darling angel,
> To fill a vacant seat.

A few blocks away, on St Patrick Street near Marchand (Louisiana 3089), a small Jewish Cemetery dates to 1856. Several graves in a cluster hold immigrants from Alsace-Lorraine, each having died in their early twenties, days apart, in the lethal Yellow Jack summer of 1878. Yellow fever was often called "the Stranger's Disease" as it preyed heaviest on new arrivals who never had the chance to acquire immunity.

From Marchand Street, turn left before the bridge onto Louisiana

308 for a lovely view of the bayou on the way out of town. Stay on this road, and you'll pass Belle Alliance (private). Enormous sasanqua, oaks, and magnolias accent the faded grandeur of this beautiful home built in 1846 as the centerpiece of a German diplomat's seven-thousand-acre sugar-cane plantation.

If, instead, you cross the bridge over to Louisiana 1 a mile out of Donaldsonville, then pause at St. Jude of the Bayou Shrine, a family-built modern chapel dedicated to the patron saint of lost causes. And that route also passes plantations: the 1850 Creole cottage Palo Alto and then the 1847 Greek Revival St. Emma, in whose cane fields hundreds died during a Civil War battle.

Either way, make sure you're back on Louisiana 1 by **Paincourtville** (PAN-ker-vil) and St. Elizabeth Catholic Church. We know what you're thinking: not another Gothic church! But this one, seemingly too big and ornate for such a tiny village, is regal. Completed in 1902, its twin spires toppled in the hurricane of 1909, never to be replaced. Inside a fanciful central pulpit stares down at hand-carved divided pews. Fantastic murals cover every inch of wall and ceiling. From the center aisle, notice high above you the engrossing depictions of the Great Heresies as monsters.

Along Bayou Lafourche, centuries of spring flooding deposited rich layers of topsoil, actually washed-away bits of Nebraska and Illinois and other states. Land concessions along the bayou gave each settler some bayou frontage for home and fields, some midrange land behind it to pasture livestock, and some wild, swampy backlands for hunting and logging. The bayou was an avenue to mercantile boats and show-boats, fishermen's pirogues (shallow-draft canoes), and the family skiff. Sunday meant a fleet moored before the church. As late as the 1930s, a courting-age girl might sit on a bayouside bench her daddy built to announce her availability. Curious boys would paddle by, but serious suitors would row, better to show off muscles.

Times have changed, of course, but you still see pirogues on the bayou. Farms are still measured in arpents, not acres. And among many old-timers, French is still the primary language.

Approaching **Napoleonville**, look for two landmarks of note. On the bayouside is Politz's Restaurant, a long-time local favorite. Next comes the graceful brick arches of Christ Episcopal Church, consecrated by "Fighting Bishop" Leonidas Polk in the 1850s. Like many of the ornate but empty businesses of downtown Napoleonville, the church is but a reminder of how wealthy the town was back when sugar was king.

An interesting detour south of town is Louisiana 401, leading ten miles back from the bayou to Attakapas Landing on cypress-fringed Lake Verret. It's a pretty spot for wild swamp scenery, often used as a backdrop for TV commercials.

Otherwise, cross the bayou at Napoleonville to Louisiana 308. A few miles downstream is enormous Madewood Plantation designed by Henry Howard, the same architect of Nottaway, in the popular 1840s Greek Revival style. Especially noteworthy are its imposing Doric columns, outdoor brick kitchen, and family cemetery. No time for a tour? Take a minute to turn down its side road to admire its lovely rear facade as well as the historic buildings recently moved there.

Five miles south of Madewood, just past one of those roadside emporia of cement statues, look for three near-identical two-story homes placed side by side. Erected in the 1920s, they are fine examples of bought-by-mail-order Sears, Roebuck & Co. houses.

Just north of **Labadieville** is the unmarked battlefield where in 1862 Cajun General Alfred Mouton led his Confederate troops to defeat trying to halt the Union invasion down Bayou Lafourche. In Labadieville proper, cross back to Louisiana 1 in front of the strikingly pretty St. Philomene Catholic Church, then continue south to the E.D. White State Commemorative Area. White spent twenty seven years on the U.S. Supreme Court, the last eleven as its chief justice, but even if he hadn't, this exemplary 1790 raised Creole cottage is easily worth the stop.

In **Thibodaux**, Politz's main restaurant is the place locals recommend for lip-smacking meals. Past strip malls and newer restaurants, turn in at Jean Lafitte National Park Wetlands Acadian Cultural Center for brochures, including one on an excellent walking tour. The Center's free museum offers a good overview of traditional bayou life.

From the Wetlands Center, turn left on Jackson, heading towards the bayou. Next, turn right onto West Third Street through old downtown to the 1862 courthouse designed by workaholic Henry Howard (though the wings, portico, and five copper domes were added much later). A right on Green Street leads to Canal Boulevard and St. Joseph Cathedral. Definitely go in for a look.

Begun in 1920, this mix of Gothic, Renaissance, and Baroque styles is elaborate with ornamental plasterwork and marble. The thirty-four-foot baldachin above the main altar is mesmerizing. Not to be missed is the glass coffin reliquary in the left nave. Its wax figure with human hair conceals a bone believed to have belonged to St. Valerie, a virgin martyr beheaded by the Romans.

Thibodaux was once an important water link from Bayou Lafourche into Bayou Terrebonne. The latter is now hidden in huge culverts under the median of Canal Boulevard. As Canal becomes Louisiana 20 toward Houma, plantation houses face the now-hidden bayou: Armitage, an 1852 Creole cottage, and Ducros, an 1833 Louisiana colonial (both private). Where Louisiana 20 climbs over the Southern Pacific tracks, hidden in the trees to the right is 1875 Wauburn Plantation. In the long, low building behind it, crawfish, frogs, and crickets from the nearby swamp are preserved and packed for lab dissection in high schools nationwide.

Louisiana 20 peels off toward Morgan City, but stay straight onto Louisiana 24. Where Bayou Terrebonne finally surfaces and splits the road, watch for the sign proclaiming "Miracles in Meat since 1891." When you walk into Bourgeois Meat Market, you'll find neither listed prices nor meat on display, but don't be alarmed. Prices are reasonable and the meat is... miraculous! All the standards are available: smoked sausage, *andouille*, as well as hard to find *boudin rouge*, a traditional blood sausage. Regular (white) *boudin* is sold cold, but their beef jerky makes great road food: lean, subtly spiced, heavily smoked, and melt-in-your-mouth tender. Although a pricey item, it is worth every bite.

At St. Bridget Catholic Church, turn right onto Louisiana 311, which soon veers left to follow Little Bayou Black and its plantations (all private). First up is 1834 Greek Revival Magnolia with extensive outbuildings and three-hundred-year-old oaks. Three and a half miles farther is fantastically startling Ardoyne—imagine a gingerbread house built by a giant! This Victorian Gothic colossus, set in a grove of enormous oaks, was built in the 1890s by the family still residing there.

Farther along Louisiana 311 are the 1810 Victorian Ellendale and 1834 Louisiana Colonial Crescent Farms. Into **Houma** proper is South-down Plantation Museum, a visit to which begins the next chapter.

For more information:

Iberville Parish/Plaquemine Tourism 800-233-3560
    P.O. Box 248, Plaquemine, LA 70765
Dow Chemical Company 504-353-6623
    P.O. Box 150, Plaquemine, LA 70765-0150
Old Turnerville Bed and Breakfast 504-687-5337
    23230 Nadler Street, Plaquemine, LA 70764
Nottaway Plantation Restaurant and Inn 504-545-2730
    P.O. Box 160, White Castle, LA 70788
Ascension Parish/Donaldsonville Tourism 504-675-6550
    6470 Highway 22, Suite A, Sorrento, LA 70778
Madewood Plantation Bed and Breakfast 504-369-7151
    4250 Highway 308, Napoleonville, LA 70390
Lafourche Parish/Thibodaux Tourist Commission 504-537-5800
    P.O. Box 340, Raceland, LA 70394
Wetlands Acadian Culture Center 504-448-1375
    314 St. Mary Street, Thibodaux, LA 70301
Houma-Terrebonne Tourist Commission 800-688-2732
    1702 St. Charles Street, P.O. Box 2792, Houma, LA 70361

CHAPTER 13
THE OLD
SPANISH TRAIL

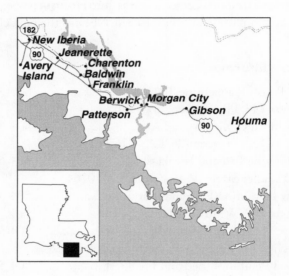

 rom **HOUMA to NEW IBERIA** on U.S. Route 90 and Louisiana 182, a hundred miles along Bayous Black and Teche, plus a final fourteen-mile spur to Avery Island. Features plantations, swamps, sugar and rice mills, and bayou villages.

The old bayou-facing courthouse with its shady square and flanking historic business district in **Houma** forms the hub from which a bicycle wheel of bridges and bayous spoke. Northwest lie grand plantations. Along the fan of bayous south and east, Cajun and Houma Indian fishing villages are picturesque with shrimp and oyster boats.

Venture to Chauvin in April for its unforgettable Blessing of the Fleet or follow Louisiana 57 down to Cocodrie, "the end of the world," to charter a boat for deep-sea fishing. While there, tour the salt-water aquariums of Lumcon marine-research facility with its wetlands observation tower.

If towns were people, Houma, founded on sugar cane, would be some eccentric inventor, always trying something new. As the southernmost rail link between Florida and Texas, it became a gateway for products of the coastal estuaries. Trappers supplied furs. Hunters brought waterfowl—iced up, they shipped nationwide by the boxcarload. By 1920, Houma was "America's Oyster Capital" while sun-dried shrimp created an export trade to China. Then came oil. In the fast and furious 1970s, helicopter flights to offshore oil rigs turned Houma's old blimp base (built to spot Nazi U-boats during World War II) into Louisiana's third busiest airport.

Leaving downtown on U.S. Route 90 west, turn right onto Louisiana 311. Across Little Bayou Black rise the old greenhouses of the State Sugarcane Experiment Station where cane species are yet perfected for maximum production and resistance to pests. A mile farther, green and pink Southdown Plantation struts from its oak trees. Southdown is the eastern end of an Anglo archipelago across the underbelly of French-speaking south Louisiana. When cane replaced indigo as the principal crop, Southdown's extensive landholdings established its owners among Louisiana's largest sugar barons. Now, its stately rooms and unique stained glass of sugar-cane motifs are a local-history museum. Folklife from 1890 to 1940 themes the Memories of Terrebonne exhibit, which the authors are quite proud of having designed, as it won a national award. To get to the house, take a left at the first light, St. Charles Street.

Farther down St. Charles is the Houma-Terrebonne Tourist Bureau. If swamp tours tempt you, pick up brochures for the several offered off the route ahead. In warm weather, some guides virtually guarantee alligator sightings, with certain big reptiles trained to come to their call.

From the tourist bureau, cross Big Bayou Black bridge and turn onto U.S. Route 90 west, the Old Spanish Trail. Hugging the bayous and cutting through swamps, this is probably the oldest route from Texas to New Orleans. When it was a cattle-drive trail, cowboys crossed streams by latching onto their swimming horse's tails. Entrepreneurial settlers made money by training a bull to swim a bayou, then renting him to lead cattle-drive herds across.

U.S. Route 90 along Big Bayou Black is a mix of old and new. Climate-controlled, spacious brick homes with docks and boat sheds give way to wood frame cottages with gardens and pirogues.

At Greenwood School, cross the bridge and continue west for two and two tenths miles to Wildlife Gardens. This hidden-away gem offers a ninety-minute guided walking tour with a hands-on, get-to-know-thy-swamp approach to native flora and fauna. Identifying blooms in season, meeting a pet nutria (kind of like a twenty-pound hamster), holding baby gators, and stumbling over cypress knees on the way to a trapper's cabin are all part of the gardens' magic.

Rental cabins built over the swamp even come with personal pirogues. Make overnight reservations in advance, especially during the spring when purple wild iris turn the swamp into a Monet painting.

Cross the next bridge back to U.S. Route 90 to continue westward. Three miles farther, an unmarked fork makes bearing left the obvious choice, but don't do it! Stay right alongside tranquil Big Bayou Black's moss-hung banks and duckweed-swashed waters.

This is **Gibson**, once a strategic railroad transshipment point called Tigerville for the panthers that stalked its untamed swamps. The isolated village's 1849 church flanks a graveyard where an 1860s brick mausoleum is the odd tomb among Anglo headstones. At the bridge, a graceful old store watches its replacement bustle across the way.

The bayouside road curls back into U.S. Route 90 onward to **Morgan City**. Interrupting the heron-crowded, road-swallowing swamp, sprawling fabrication yards build offshore oil rigs. From the highway, they'd pass for Tinker Toys except that ant-sized human workers give them scale.

Go-go bars, scrap yards, and supply docks provide an inauspicious welcome to Morgan City. Born as Brashear in the 1850s when the Louisiana and Texas Railroad got no closer to Texas than here, this port boomed after the drilling of the first deep-water offshore oil well in 1947. About the same time a growing fleet of deep-draft shrimp trawlers began to call the city home. Together, the two industries heralded a roughhewn prosperity, until the near-collapse of the local oil business after 1982. But Morgan City perseveres, and its annual Labor Day Shrimp and Petroleum Festival is a jam-packed music and food blowout, complete with boat parade.

On Myrtle Street, next to the Civic Center, the Morgan City Tourist Center offers entree to its funky "swamp gardens" next door as well as helpful area brochures. In old downtown, along the waterfront, an enormous sea wall is a contemporary bas-relief of local scenes; and the Turn-of-the-Century House Museum near Lawrence Park recreates an upper-middle-class family home.

Crossing the Atchafalaya River, U.S. Route 90 literally passes over Berwick. Founded in 1797, it was overshadowed long ago by its east-bank rival. Four miles farther, watch for the turnoff onto Louisiana 182. At the Atchafalaya Delta Visitors Center, you can pick up info on the many plantations you'll be seeing, including which offer tours. The restful vista of Bayou Teche inspires lingering; no need, the upcoming drive is rich with such views.

Louisiana 182, still the Old Spanish Trail (more readily known to our generation as "Old Highway 90") skips into **Patterson**. Here was once the world's largest cypress lumber mill, fed by thousand-year-old trees floated from the surrounding swamps. By the late 1920s, most of the old-growth forest was gone.

The road winds back to rejoin U.S. Route 90 across the Wax Lake Outlet, a flood spillway that doubles as a navigation canal. Past the bridge, turn back onto Louisiana 182.

Steamboat landings that became lumber boom towns have gone back to being sleepy villages; places like **Centerville** and **Garden**

City, where the Garden City Store, established 1938, upholds its general merchandise tradition by selling food, sundries, new-age herbal remedies, and an eclectic mix of castoffs and collectibles.

A short drive farther, picture-book pretty **Franklin** opens its arms with "the Great White Way," a double row of oak-shaded mansions. Ornamental lamp posts lead to a bustling downtown that dates mostly from the lumber-boom era, starting with the railroad's arrival in 1879. But some structures go back as far as the 1830s.

In the Civil War, the town changed hands repeatedly, complete with house-to-house fighting. Confederates scuttled a gunboat, trying to block the bayou; they failed. Union troops tried to burn the town; thankfully they failed too. By the fall of 1863, when General Banks led his federal troops through on the "Great Texas Overland Expedition" (which would fail as well), Franklin residents had taken to decking their homes with the flags of France, England, Spain—even Prussia—in hopes that the claim of foreign nationality might keep them safe from either side's combatants.

To discover how upper-crust town folk lived back then, follow Louisiana 182 through old downtown to Louisiana 322. The Frances Grevemberg House Museum was built for a woman widowed by the tragic 1856 Last Island Hurricane which erased a fashionable coastal resort and with it many of Louisiana's wealthy elite. Despite marble mantels, faux-bois detailing, and fancy wallpaper (a detail most period restorations forget), the house is simple in its grandeur.

Leaving the Grevemberg Museum, continue out Louisiana 322 past the Sterling Sugar Mill. During "grinding season" (October to December), beware the rumbling, top-heavy cane trucks, but also pause for a glance at the sugar mountain under the bayouside dome.

Louisiana 322 follows Bayou Teche's Irish Bend through swishing cane. Apart from harvest time, it's a place of such rural quiet that it's hard to imagine how very bloody a battle was fought across these fields in spring of 1862. The roadside relic Medric Martin Grocery, seemingly in the middle of nowhere, is a perfect thirst-quenching stop.

A couple of miles farther is Oaklawn Manor, home of Louisiana

Governor Mike Foster. Only the ground floor is open for tours, but the Venetian, Baccarat, and former Jockey Club of New Orleans chandeliers, along with extensive Audubon prints, decoy collections, and ornate interiors, are impressively ostentatious. What treasures must the upper floors, including a third-floor ballroom, hold?

A short ride farther, Louisiana 322 bumps into Louisiana 182. A right leads onward to **Baldwin**. St. Mary's Bank, at 102 Main Street, occupies the West Indies-style 1827 Darby House—a welcome simplicity after Greek Revival overload. Its upstairs porch shows an example of *bousillage* (plaster of Spanish moss and mud) construction.

Just past Baldwin, a right on Louisiana 326 ventures toward **Charenton** and the Chitimacha Indian Reservation. The visitors center exhibits the tribe's famous and rare double-weave baskets as well as a video documentary. But the reservation's most visited site is Cypress Bayou Casino, one of those enormous slot-machine and gaming parlors that threaten to become what people most associate with Native American culture. To try your luck, simply follow the signs.

Louisiana 326 traipses through woods back to sugar-cane-lined Louisiana 182 where westward lies a favorite country restaurant. The Yellow Bowl just east of **Jeanerette** didn't have to worry when a newer highway bypassed them, such was their fame and loyalty among the motoring public. Unpretentious Cajun home cooking, fried seafood, and generous helpings draw serious Louisiana food lovers who consider driving hours just to eat here in no way eccentric.

Jeanerette itself is framed by sugar mills. In between are antique shops, terrific old buildings, and the Beau Petit Musée, a museum emphasizing the area's two-hundred-year history of sugar-cane farming and bayou life.

In an embarrassment of culinary riches so near to the Yellow Bowl, Jeanerette also has LeJeune's Bakery where perhaps the world's best French bread comes hot from the oven around 11:00 A.M. Use the side entrance of 1510 Main Street, order in French if you prefer, and don't pass up the delectable, gingery stage planks when available. And don't wait for the first bite to persuade you to buy extra! Yum!

Wipe away the crumbs and continue winding along the Teche. In fall, sugar-cane barges used to crowd its channel. Paddle-wheel boats regularly plied its waters supplying plantations and stores well into the 1940s. A Franklin woman remembers, "I'd paddle my pirogue into the wake of the freight boat. It'd pull me clear to New Iberia. Free ride."

Entering **New Iberia**, drive slowly past beaucoup mansions (including Shadows-on-the-Teche) to park in downtown's central lot. From a pedestal gazes a bust of Francisco de Bouligny, colonial founder of Nueva Iberia (New Spain). But if you like statuary, New Iberia's glory is up Weeks Street where a genuine two-thousand-year-old larger-than-life statue of Roman Emperor Hadrian lords over a bank. Go figure.

Victor's Cafeteria on Main Street, with its pressed-tin ceilings, finds the town's old guard and young turks debating the price of oil, the sugar subsidy, and the weather. A few blocks farther on Iberia Street is a fun stretch of antique shops.

After strolling the fancy tiled entryways of Main Street's shops and browsing the latest bestsellers at Books Along the Teche, return to the Shadows-on-the-Teche. A gracious antebellum manor nestled amid peaceful gardens on the bayou's banks, it was restored to its 1840s elegance by descendant Weeks Hall who discovered antiquities in the attic accumulated by four generations. The only National Trust home in Louisiana, its forty-five-minute guided, interpretive tour is well worth it.

A more unusual stop in New Iberia is the Rosary House at 699 East St. Peter (parallels Main). It's an appropriate address, since this is a factory outlet for religious articles of every magnitude. Even amidst aisle after aisle of articles of faith, we confess to feeling devilishly fascinated as we stood with shopping baskets on our arms having the helpful staff direct us to the patron saints appropriate to our names, professions, and afflictions. The statuary store next door, with Jesus de Milo on its façade, only wholesales.

The Konriko Company Store and Rice Mill lies just catty-cornered across Ann Street and the railroad tracks. Though it may seem oddly

Blue crab

placed in the heart of sugar country, Vermilion Parish rice farms are actually not that far away. This is the grandpappy of rice-mill tours, complete with a slide show and mega-gift shop stuffed with souvenirs and the wafting aroma of tempting food samples. In ample supply, naturally, is Konriko's own tasty line of packaged rice dishes.

Of course, for more than a century, no serious tourist visits New Iberia without a side trip to **Avery Island**, south on Louisiana 329. This broad, marsh-bound hill is actually a salt dome that's been mined since before the Civil War. But what made Avery Island famous is Tabasco, and that grande dame of hot sauces is aged and bottled right here. Free plant tours start from the visitors center and end at the nifty gift shop.

The two-hundred-acre adjacent Jungle Gardens are beautiful during spring blooms, especially if you take time to rove the twisting pathways. Don't miss the raucous Snowy Egret sanctuary or the centuries-old Buddha set amid mossy trees in a lush natural setting of native plants. Back on U.S. Route 90, west of the Louisiana 14 intersection is a seafood mecca in a region where driving the "farthest for the freshest" has become more than a motto. The Guiding Star seasons its boiled crawfish (December to May) and blue crabs (after May) with a secret mix of spices and Tabasco pepper mash (the same stuff they use to put the "heat" in Ben-Gay). The rest of the menu is a tried-and-true list of Cajun specialties. Just remember: If you order the boiled seafood, don't touch any sensitive areas with your peppery fingers afterwards!

For more information:

Southdown Plantation 504-851-0154
    Highway 311 at St. Charles Street, Houma, LA 70360
Houma-Terrebonne Tourist Commission 800-688-2732
    1702 St. Charles Street, P.O. Box 2792, Houma, LA 70361
Wildlife Gardens, Gibson 504-575-3676
    5306 North Bayou Black Drive, Gibson, LA 70356
Morgan City Tourist Center 504-384-3343
    725 Myrtle Street, Morgan City, LA 70380
St. Mary/Atchafalaya Delta Visitors Center 800-256-2931
    P.O. Box 2332, Morgan City, LA 70381
Iberia Parish Tourist Commission 318-365-1540
    2704 Highway 14, New Iberia, LA 70560
Konriko Company Store & Rice Mill 318-364-7242
    307 Ann Street, New Iberia, LA 70560
Shadows-on-the-Teche Manor House 318-369-6446
    317 East Main, New Iberia, LA 70560
Avery Island/TabascoVisitors Information 800-634-9599
    Avery Island, LA 70513

CHAPTER 14
CRAWFISH
AND BOUDIN

 rom **LAFAYETTE to WASHINGTON** along upper Bayou Teche via St. Martinville, Breaux Bridge, and Opelousas, about seventy-five miles. Features some of Louisiana's oldest settlements, Cajun and Creole culinary delicacies, Zydeco dancing, native flowers, and antiques.

It's merely coincidence that this chapter starts and ends in towns named for heroes of the American Revolution. During that 1776 brouhaha, upper Bayou Teche was a faraway Spanish precinct being settled by sundry French-speaking peoples. Our route was trekked back then by the lowly administrator, marginal peddler, and even an occasional struggling troupe of actors trying to milk a date in la Nouvelle Orléans with visits to the diversion-hungry frontier *postes* of Opelousas and Attakapas.

Southeast of **Lafayette**, Pinhook Road becomes Louisiana 182 as it darts through **Broussard**, where suburbia encroaches on handsome Victorian mansions. Drifting into countryside, a left on Louisiana 96 leads to **St. Martinville** through atypical rolling terrain. These *côteaux* (ridges) are the rough edges of the flat southwest Louisiana prairies crumbling into the lower but equally flat alluvial plain of the Mississippi Valley.

In St. Martinville, Louisiana 96 meets Main Street. Straight ahead, on Bayou Teche, the huge and hugely famous Evangeline Oak shades sidewalk musicians and storytellers. Next to it, the Old Castillo Hotel and Restaurant, an 1840s steamboat inn, once again accommodates overnighters. Homey restaurants and well-frequented stores frame la Place d'Evangéline. Its namesake statue, next to St. Martin de Tours Catholic Church, is actually the likeness of Delores Del Rio. The silent movie star portrayed Evangeline in the 1929 film partly shot here. The neighboring Petit Paris Museum has an extensive costume display and recounts local history when St. Martinville, the *poste des Attakapas*, was as near to civilization as settlers got, earning it the name "Petit Paris."

Though St. Martinville's French heritage actually owes more to mainland France and Haiti, its cult of Evangeline celebrates the Acadians' poignant story. Landing in North America before the Pilgrims, Acadian settlements in eastern Canada halfway between New England and New France eventually proved too strategic for their own good. In 1755, the British scattered the French-speakers into exile. On Louisiana's bayous, many reunited and prospered.

Borrowing the plot from his buddy Nathaniel Hawthorne, Henry Wadsworth Longfellow published *Evangeline* in 1847. The epic tearjerker of star-crossed Acadian lovers became a runaway best seller. When tourists started showing up to see the oak where Evangeline awaited her Gabriel, St. Martinville was more than happy to oblige.

A mile west on Louisiana 31 (Main Street), Arceneaux/Olivier Plantation graces the Longfellow-Evangeline Commemorative Area. The 1820s raised cottage and nearby Acadian settler's cabin offer contrasting glimpses of long-ago daily life. And the guide will fill your ears with stories of the "real" Evangeline and Gabriel.

Louisiana 31 continues to Breaux Bridge, but we wanted to take the scenic route. Back at the church square, Louisiana 96 (Bridge Street) appropriately enough crosses Bayou Teche. For many, this is the route to Lake Fausse Pointe State Park. With hiking, fishing, cabins, and campsites, its six thousand acres on the very edge of the vast Atchafalaya Swamp rate it among Louisiana's prettiest public parks. From Louisiana 96, it's about fifteen miles east. Go right on Louisiana 679, left on Louisiana 3083, then right on Levee Road.

Considerably closer, two miles north of St. Martinville on Louisiana 96 is majestic Pine Oak Alley. Our occasional partner in mischief, Sprinky Durand, tells how an ancestor owned the "big house" to which this mile-long arbor once led.

"For a daughter's wedding, he imported spiders from China and turned them loose in the trees. On the eve of the ceremony, he had each and every web sprinkled with gold dust. It must have been spectacular," Sprinky proclaims, staring down the alley as if the live oak and pine branches were still aglitter. "Of course, it also helps explain why the family fortune never made it down to me."

Two miles farther, the road takes a sharp curve right. Instead, turn left onto the parish road through rustling fields of swaying cane to connect with Louisiana 347 at the giant peaked sugar hangar of Levert-St. John Plantation. To the left, impressive gates set off the Greek Revival big house (private). To the right are the plantation store and office. Next to the mill, follow St. John Bridge Road over a precariously quaint one-car-at-a-time bridge. It's an interesting up-close look at a plantation mill complex, but from the October-to-December grinding season be very careful (and courteous) of the cane wagons.

Across Bayou Teche, turn right on Louisiana 31 to **Breaux Bridge**,

Cajun house

a town world famous for its Crawfish Festival. Started in 1959 as a biennial downtown affair, like the popularity of crawfish, the fete grew so big and so rowdy that now it's held every May and on the outskirts

of town. Other times (especially during the December-to-May crawfish season) a noteworthy culinary detour is east to the seafood and
swamp-tour heaven of **Henderson**, where Interstate 10 starts its
twenty-mile causeway over America's largest river swamp.

At the light in downtown Breaux Bridge, where patrons find shade
beneath the old galleried storefronts and bars, cross the Bayou Teche
bridge that gave the town its name. Jog right to take Louisiana 347
out past La Poussière ("The Dust," as in what dancers kick up), a
regionally famous old-fashioned dance hall. When the Interstate 10
overpass comes in sight, you're there.

Straight ahead (north of Interstate 10) is Landry's, its large restaurant enlivened by attached galleries and gift shops aimed squarely at
the interstate trade. Past it, Crawfish Town USA is the spot for pinch-
the-tails, suck-the-heads, never-forget-and-put-your-peppery-fingers-
in-your-eye quantity eating.

Or avoid most tour buses by turning onto Louisiana 352 (south of
Interstate 10) toward the levee. On the left will be Robin's (RO-
banz), to our mind home to the best *étouffée* and bisque. The subtle
aromas alone make it worth the stop. At the end of the road, beside
the levee, Pat's Fisherman's Wharf is the joint that sired all the others; in the evenings, one dines on its screened porch to the music of
crickets and bullfrogs.

Swamp tours depart from several well-marked spots along the levee.
We prefer the one of our old friends the Allemand family that launches
from McGee's Landing. But with such a pretty patch of swamp, it's
hard to go wrong. In the spring, high water ferries you to places less
accessible at other times. Herons build nests, moss (actually a brome-
liad) is tinged green, and fleeting blooms drift among cypress knees.
The Atchafalaya is a mysterious forest primeval.

Back in Breaux Bridge, weave north through town on Louisiana
31. At Louisiana 94, a quarter mile left is Mulate's where Cajun
music accompanies country cooking evenings and weekend after-
noons. The success of this family restaurant-cum-dance-hall con-
cept spawned numerous imitators as well as larger, grander branches
in Baton Rouge and New Orleans, but this is the original. In spite

of enlargements and tour buses, locals still jump up between courses to waltz or two-step to live Cajun music. It's as close as most visitors will ever get to an old-time Cajun *fais do-do*. Meaning a ball or dance, literally *fais do-do* is baby talk for "go to sleep"; in an age before baby-sitters, that's what you had to keep telling the little ones you'd brought along with you.

Northbound again on Louisiana 31, it's four miles past Interstate 10 to Poche's (PO-shays). The standard lunch menu of succulent pork steak, barbecue, and to-die-for crawfish *étouffée* is supplemented by daily specials like smothered rabbit ("smothered" referring to the manner of cooking, not the mode of death). The attached grocery and meat market features spiced Cajun sausages: lean *andouille*, peppery *chourice*, and smoked *saucisse boucannée*. Other delicacies are *tasso* (lean beef or pork, marinated, then smoked), *ponce* (stuffed pig stomach), and piping hot *boudin* (rice and pork sausage).

Taste buds dancing, we staggered to our Plymouth to cache our loot in the cooler. Ambling north, moss-draped oaks, old barns, and sugar cane fields sidle along Louisiana 31 until **Arnaudville**. There, to the right, zigzagging over bridges that span the junction of Bayous Fusilier and Teche, is Arnaudville proper and nearby **Leonville**, the cultural heartland for southwest Louisiana's Creoles of color.

Turning left before the Arnaudville bridge, Louisiana 93 west sashays through pretty cattle and horse farms, the scattered houses often surrounded with old-style whitewashed shade trees. Bearded oaks multiply as Louisiana 93 enters **Grand Coteau**. St. Charles College's parklike campus invites crawling past for a view. Turn right onto Church Street (Louisiana 760-1) where a Catholic church, school, and retreat house (complete with outdoor stations of the cross) reassert this very old community's foundation of Catholicism.

The road curves under oak and pine alleys to the three-story main building of Academy of the Sacred Heart. Fronted with formal gardens, its delicate cast-iron columns support graceful lace-work balconies. For the forty-five-minute guided tour of the chapel, the site of the St. John Berchmans miracle, and the delightful museum tracing schooling here since 1821, you'll need to call in advance, but even drop-in visitors are free to stroll the gardens.

Follow Louisiana 93 west under Interstate 49 then turn right onto Louisiana 182. In **Sunset**, stop at Dugas' for a cup of steaming coffee strong enough to revive any traveler. A daily plate lunch of country cooking is geared to hearty appetites. Dugas's sign proclaims its six tables and lunch counter open for "breakfast and dinner," but be warned: Dinner means Cajun dinner, the noon meal, not evening "supper."

Nearby Chretien Point Plantation offers a pleasant detour. Ignore the signs that lead down Louisiana 93; there's a more scenic route ahead off Louisiana 182. First stop at Rowena's Market for great *boudin* (who makes the best *boudin* is a bigger rivalry than football between certain Cajun towns) and tasty *pistolettes* (small rolls stuffed with meat or crawfish). A mile farther, turn left onto Louisiana 754, then left again onto Parish Road 2-151. Skip right to pass rows of tiny metal A-frame fighting-cock coops lined up like graves in a military cemetery. Cross a small bridge over the shrouded upper reaches of Bayou Queue de Tortue, then saunter through the cane fields to the classic 1831 Greek Revival house used as the inspiration for the movie version of *Gone with the Wind*'s Tara. The elegant home offers tours and a bed and breakfast.

Back on Louisiana 182, old homes interrupt horse farms the five and a half miles to Louisiana Nursery. We first heard of this place from a lily fiend/friend in Beverly Hills. Here, on the outskirts of Opelousas is North America's largest mail-order nursery for iris and daylilies. Over five thousand varieties of plants spread across fifty-six acres of arboretum, greenhouses, and iris ponds. Many hybrids have Louisiana names like Zydeco and Chicot, creations the Durio family proudly claims. Potted plants are available for purchase; order anything else in advance so it can be dug up. Even if you aren't looking to take plants home, a spring day's visit, especially late February through June, is a spectacular bloom-filled reward.

Entering **Opelousas**, you soon reach U.S. Route 190, the main east-west thoroughfare. A few blocks west is the Art Deco courthouse and, across the street, the landmark Palace Cafe where for over a half century the local courthouse gang has been cutting deals. The Palace's cuisine is worthy of such intrigue, simple on the surface, but as full of flavorful nuance as a country politician's stump speech promise. The honey-sweet baklava is especially wonderful and not some trendy new addition—they've been making it for decades.

East on U.S. Route 190 is the helpful visitors center. Driving- and walking-tour brochures of Opelousas will satisfy any vintage home appetite; museums include a local-history interpretive center and a fire-fighting collection. Opelousas' 1809 Michel Prudhomme house is especially nice, but even the old buildings clustered around the visitors center provide an interesting stroll. Across the street, at the drive-thru window next to the cool pistol-packing sausage sign, order a couple of hot links of Ray's excellent homemade *boudin*.

Louisiana's third oldest city, Opelousas was founded as a trading post in 1720 by Canadian *coureurs de bois*. Once home to Jim Bowie, of knife and Alamo fame, in 1838 it was briefly the residence of famous showman P.T. Barnum, whose freak show went broke here. Disbanding his entertainers (his star attraction was an allegedly 162-year-old-woman), he traded his showboat for a cargo of local molasses and returned to New York to begin anew.

Union Street bends around the 1908 Romanesque St. Landry Church to join Main Street. (Farther north, it becomes Louisiana 10 east.) Near the edge of town is Slim's Y-Ki-Ki, a great place to dance and listen to some hot Zydeco music if you're spending a weekend night.

Zydeco is the music of Louisiana's French-speaking Afro-Caribbean culture. The name comes from a song title, "Les Haricots Sont Pas Salés" (The Snap Beans Aren't Salty), reflecting the music's relation to the blues. Hard times indeed when there was no salt pork to flavor a pot of haricots! Richard's, a few miles west on U.S. Route 190 at **Lawtell**, is another big, famous, visitor-friendly Zydeco club. Smaller clubs abound.

Louisiana 10 east leads to **Washington**, an 1800s steamboat port that has re-created itself as a bed and breakfast and antique destination. A local museum/tourist center at Main and Dejean Streets offers history, bed-and-breakfast and home-tour information. Take time to weave through the lovely streets past one charming house after another. If the thought of so many antique and flea markets sets your heart aflutter, then make sure you arrive on the weekend— many shops close during the week—and don't forget the Antique School Mall. Off Vine Street a few blocks east of Main, both the two-story school and gym are chock-a-block full of collectibles.

Serving tasty adaptations of local cuisine, Washington's upscale Steamboat Restaurant is in an original bayouside warehouse. It once held cotton bales from the fall harvest until spring high water allowed paddle wheelers up Bayou Courtableau to collect them. If you're in more of a hurry than that, from the light on Main Street, Louisiana 103 goes east to Interstate 49 or west to Ville Platte and the Cajun prairies of the next chapter.

For more information:

St. Martinville Tourism Commission 318-394-7578
    P.O. Box 379, St. Martinville, LA 70582
Old Castillo Hotel 800-621-3017
    220 Evangeline Boulevard, St. Martinville, LA 70582
Breaux Bridge Chamber of Commerce 318-332-5406
    111 Rees Street, Breaux Bridge, LA 70517
McGee's Landing 318-228-2384
    1337 Henderson Levee Road, Breaux Bridge, LA 70517
Academy of the Sacred Heart 318-662-5275
    1821 Academy Road, Grand Coteau, LA 70541
Chretien Point Plantation 800-880-7050
    U.S. Route 1, Box 162, Sunset, LA 70584
St. Landry / Opelousas /
    Washington Tourist Information 800-424-5442
    P.O. Box 1415, Opelousas, LA 70570-1415

Slim's Y-Ki-Ki Zydeco Dancehall 318-942-9980
    U.S. Route 167 North, Opelousas 70570
Louisiana Nursery 318-948-3696
    U.S. Route 7, Box 43, Opelousas, LA 70570

CHAPTER 15

THE CAJUN PRAIRIES

rom **WASHINGTON to LAFAYETTE** via Ville Platte, Eunice, Jennings and Crowley, about a hundred and twenty-five miles. Features rice, Cajun music, Mardi Gras, Native American crafts, antiques, Victorian houses, old masters paintings, and *boudin*.

From the Main Street antique shops of **Washington** (or if you prefer, the Washington exit of Interstate 49) take Louisiana 103 west toward Grand Prairie and switch the radio to an early-morning "French music" show (what Cajuns called their music before the rest of the world discovered it). As an acrobatic fiddle melody rides bucking accordion rhythms, the pretty road snakes past Bayou Carron plantations before turning to meet U.S. Route 167.

Turn right, toward Ville Platte, and watch as roadside fields start to show the telltale low, curved levees of rice farms. Our journey is across southwest Louisiana's prairies that stretch to the Gulf beyond the southern limit of the South's vast forests of pine.

But first comes **Ville Platte**. Follow the signs to Floyd's Record Shop, an emporium for just about every CD and cassette ever made by a Cajun, Zydeco, or Swamp Pop artist. (And yes, even stacks of LPs and 45s tucked away in back!) Owner Floyd Soileau not only sells records, he makes them and has for decades, even back when Cajun music was derided as "chanky-chank" and Zydeco was "Colored French music."

Just half a block from Floyd's is The Pig Stand, more of a sit-down restaurant than the name implies. Its tradition of hearty breakfasts, lunches, and dinners make it Ville Platte's most cherished eatery, though crawfish at the Jungle Club on West Main Street offers dinner-time competition.

Before sailing out onto the prairies, we took a short side trip north to say goodbye to the woods. Seven miles out Louisiana 3042 is Chicot (CHEE-ko) State Park with cabins, campsites, and hiking trails. Boat rentals give even tourists a shot at catching their limit in two-thousand-acre Chicot Lake. In Cajun, *chicot* means stump, so as you might expect it's a woodsy, overgrown fishing hole, fun to explore even when nothing's biting.

Adjacent to the park (its main entrance is a mile farther on Louisiana 3042) is the free Louisiana State Arboretum where well-marked trails cover six hundred acres of hilly forest filled with magnolia, dogwood, and many other identified native species.

Back in Ville Platte, take Louisiana 10 west onto the prairie. Ten miles out, at a four-way stop, turn south onto Louisiana 13 toward Mamou and Eunice. Along with the trees, you've left behind the bayou roads of French-surveyed southeast Louisiana and the ridge roads of

English-surveyed north Louisiana. The prairies were mapped on the American system, a regular grid of townships and ranges. To go south or west, the route is arrow straight; but to go southwest requires zigzags.

Partly because of natural fires, partly because of a clay layer a few feet down that hindered drainage, there was no forest primeval here except for the narrow bands of trees that grew along streams. In between, seas of grasses like bluestem, switchgrass and broomsedge, some growing six feet tall, flourished. Seasonal wildflowers elbowed for room. In the 1760s, Cajuns from posts at Opelousas and St. Martinville began moving into the area. They settled in the *anses* (coves) along the prairies' wooded edges. For more than a century, the vast flat grasslands were left for cattle to range, hunters to stalk, and outlaws to hide in.

Take a left onto Louisiana 104 following the signs into **Mamou**. The town's fame rests on enjoying its good times a bit differently. For instance, Mamou's big Saturday Cajun dance, a tradition for decades, is held FIRST THING IN THE MORNING! That's right, from 9:00 A.M. to 1:00 P.M. every Saturday since forever, Fred's Lounge crowds in locals, tourists, a Cajun band, and even a live radio hookup.

Mamou was also first of the prairie towns to revive the Courir de Mardi Gras, a rural carnival tradition descended from the "beggars' feast" of medieval France. Starting early Mardi Gras morning (the Tuesday before Ash Wednesday), masked and gaudily costumed horsemen comb the countryside, speaking in falsetto, dancing, singing, showing off and begging at every farmhouse that will receive them. Their performances earn rice, flour, onions, or even a live chicken which they fight each other to capture. By afternoon, collected ingredients go into a communal gumbo; music and dancing accompany the last raucous feast before Lent begins.

Nowadays, Mardi Gras is "run" in many prairie towns: Mamou, Eunice, Elton, Iota, Church Point, Scott. Visitors can (and do) line country roadsides to watch, as well as join the in-town afternoon festivities.

Louisiana 13 continues to **Eunice**. A block south of U.S. Route 190, the town's main east-west drag, the old railroad depot now contains a local museum. From it, West Park Boulevard leads to a statue of Eunice Duhon (the town's namesake by virtue of her marriage to an 1880s developer) and two primary tourist attractions. The Liberty Theatre is Saturday evenings' home to a Prairie Home Companion-esque live radio show. Entirely in Cajun French, it's very popular, so arrive early to get seats. The other is the Prairie Acadian Culture Center, a well-mounted and free interpretive museum, theater, and folk-life demonstration venue run by the National Park Service. (Glen wrote the Center's interpretive text, so we can vouch for its accuracy, insight, and wit.)

A block away on Walnut Street, Ruby's is famous for big breakfast and lunch specials. Opening at 5:00 A.M., Cajun French is lingua franca till well past sunrise. After dropping a few *bon mots*, we'd met everyone in the restaurant, heard all the latest jokes, and were discussing the rice crop's prospects. An east-side favorite, south of U.S. Route 190 on St. Mary Street, Mathilde's Barbecue and Seafood packs them in for lunch and early supper.

In the 1870s and '80s, it was the railroad that settled the prairies, bringing new peoples, new crops, new ways of living. We parallel the Missouri Pacific taking U.S. Route 190 west out of town. Ten miles of lonely farm country reach **Basile** (Bah-ZEEL) centered along the tracks a few blocks north. With Casper's Tonsorial Parlour next to Miss Bea's Cafe and the Main Street Lounge, a quintessential Cajun dance hall, Basile is the kind of town where Andy Griffith could be sheriff, if only he spoke French.

West of town, pine woods bordering Bayou Nezpique interrupt the monotony of rice fields. During the prairies' 1880s land rush, grain farmers immigrating from midwestern states discovered, as Cajuns had a century before, the local climate unsuitable for wheat and many other crops. No one knows who first realized that the prairies' notoriously poor drainage is perfect for holding the water necessary to grow rice. Cajuns had long grown rice, but it was usually "Providence" rice, so named because after planting in shallow ponds, it was abandoned to heaven until harvest time.

Acadian Village

Today, the low, curved levees of flooded rice fields create the prairies' most distinctive feature, and rice is indispensable in Cajun cooking. It's floated in soups (gumbo, bisque), covered with stews (fricassee, *étouffée*), cooked in sauces (jambalaya), buried under tomato dishes (*sauce piquante*), mixed into a dressing (*farre*) which is sometimes stuffed into sausage (*boudin*), and even sweetened into dessert (*bouillie de riz*).

Elton is a village of rice dryers and flea markets wedged against the north edge of the prairie. The Estherwood Rice Mill, across the tracks facing the big elevators, gives engaging tours of milling operations and sells gaily printed custom rice sacks that make unique gifts. Miss Lurcy's, in the middle of town, is the place to eat.

The Coushatta Tribal Center is tucked north of town way back in the pines. Turn right at the historical marker, over the tracks, veering left then right onto Parish Road 193. One-lane bridges punctuate the not-much-wider road to the gift shop, restaurant, and food store operated and owned by the tribe. This is the source for famous Coushatta pine-needle baskets, some intricately woven into fanciful animal effigies. At the small museum, friendly folk explain Coushatta history and traditions. A huge casino recently opened on tribal lands in nearby Kinder—one wonders what the future holds.

From the eastern edge of Elton, turn right on Louisiana 26 south past Lucky's Gaming Club (a cockpit arena for cockfights). The sixteen miles to **Jennings** offer more straight road, rice fields, and scattered farmhouses.

An old-timer hereabouts told us how as a child on one of these isolated farms, after supper all the kids would go "out on the porch, slapping mosquitoes, hunting the horizon for a bouncing speck of light. If we saw it, we knew to roast some coffee before the stove cooled off. See, that light was a lantern somebody'd strung on a pole above their buggy—a signal saying, *On v'etre là tal'heure pour faire la veillée*." (We'll be there soon for a little socializing.)

Jennings, Crowley, and Rayne are three small cities tethered by the Southern Pacific, U.S. Route 90, and Interstate 10. Founded by Anglos, adopted by Cajuns, they share similar history, economy, and look and will milepost our trip east to Lafayette. They also each have antique malls!

Where Louisiana 26 crosses Interstate 10, Jennings' elaborate visitors center offers info, an alligator aquarium, and a replica oil derrick—the state's first gusher spudded in near here in 1901. South off U.S. Route 90, visit spruced-up Main Street's antiques mall, shops, theater, Telephone Museum, and an engrossing time capsule called the Tupper General Merchandise Museum. A block west, Victorian homes line Cary Avenue, and off it, the Zigler Museum on Clara Street features originals by Rembrandt, Durer, Van Dyck, Whistler, and many others, including Louisiana artists.

For vittles, the Boudin King (on Division Street west of Louisiana 26) is regionally famous for... what do you think? At Donn E's (on Louisiana 26 just north of Interstate 10) we enjoyed a buffet so extensive and so tasty Glen had to undo no less than two notches of his belt.

A worthy side trip from Jennings is ten miles (of more rice fields) south on Louisiana 26 to **Lake Arthur**. A beautiful, sleepy little one-time resort where a downtown park boasts fishing piers extending into the lake. A shady lake-shore lane meanders between cypress-fringed water and fine old lake-view homes. A fat goose (wild or tame, we couldn't tell) honked at us as we drove by.

From Jennings, U.S. Route 90 leads east over the Mermentau River to **Crowley**, where it becomes 2nd Street. Five huge turn-of-the-century rice mills are what built Crowley and keep it thriving. At Parkerson Avenue (Louisiana 13) turn left into a picture-postcard downtown where locals still shop. We bought cream puffs at Ruddock's Bakery, facing the Art Deco courthouse, before turning east on Hutchinson Avenue to weave back and forth between it and the tracks (where the old depot is a visitors center), ogling perhaps the grandest, frilliest collection of Victorian houses in any Louisiana town.

Crowley's Rice Museum is open by appointment, but a much more astonishing archive lies just south of town at the Blue Rose Museum (call ahead). Follow Louisiana 13 (Eastern Avenue) south to a right on Airport Road. After two miles, a large clump of trees on the left marks Wright Enrichment Facility where vitamins and minerals from around the world are blended to enrich bread, breakfast cereal, and other foods. We arrived the day after Kellogg's had made their annual white-gloves inspection.

Next to the main office, the Blue Rose Museum is a lovely 1840s Acadian cottage built of handmade bricks, *bousillage* and cypress. Displayed inside is the Wright family's really incredible collection of china, glassware, dolls, demitasse cups, furniture, clothing, art, and whatnot items. A guaranteed dazzler even if you don't know your Wedgwood from your Noritake. If you're lucky, the family's antique cars may also be included in the tour.

Back on U.S. Route 90, **Rayne** is famed for its annual September Frog Festival and fanciful, often hilarious frog murals that seem to cover every blank exterior wall in town. This trip, we bought several links of *boudin* at Champagne's grocery (where they're happy to heat it for you), then cruised around hunting amphibian art. Other times, we've come to Rayne to comb its extensive flea markets, open every other weekend.

East of Rayne, Lafayette begins to exert a pull. Its blue laws support after-hours honky-tonks in less squeamish outlying towns. **Duson** boasts Thibodeaux's, a block north of the tracks, for crawfish, steaks, and the feel of an old-time roadhouse.

In **Scott**, what used to be an old St. Mary Street saloon now holds Floyd Sonnier's Beau Cajun Art Gallery, two blocks north of U.S. Route 90. This lauded Cajun artist's elegant prints depict rural settings and traditional lifestyles. Almost a museum unto itself for the antiques laying about, his gallery also sells T-shirts, cards, and calendars. Great gifts!

Fending off the bustle of Lafayette, we aimed for Acadian Village. Turn left on Louisiana 93 to a right on Ridge Road, following the signs. The village keeps improving with age, adding a Native American museum, more houses where ladies sit quilting, and additional intriguing artifacts. From the bridge near the church, we tossed corn to the ducks as French music lulled us, gazing at the assemblage of 1800s houses, a country tour unto itself.

For more information:

St. Landry/Washington/Eunice Tourist Commission ... 800-424-5442
  P.O. Box 1415, Opelousas, LA 70570-1415
Ville Platte Chamber of Commerce 318-363-1878
  306 West Main Street, Ville Platte, LA 70586
Floyd's Record Shop 318-363-2138
  434 East Main, Ville Platte, LA 70586
Chicot State Park 318-363-2403
  U.S. Route 2, Box 494, Ville Platte, LA 70586
City of Eunice 318-457-7389
  200 West Park Avenue, Eunice, LA 70535
Jean Lafitte Prairie Acadian Culture Center 318-457-8490
  250 West Park Avenue, Eunice, LA 70535
Estherwood Rice Mill 318-584-2391
  P.O. Box 160, Elton, LA 70532
Coushatta Tribal Center 318-584-2261
  Powell Road, P.O. Box 818, Elton, LA 70532
Jeff Davis Tourist Commission 800-264-5521
  Interstate 10, Exit 64, Jennings, LA 70546
Acadia Parish/Crowley Tourist Commission 318-783-2108
  114 East First Street, Crowley, LA 70527
Blue Rose Museum 318-783-3096
  Wright Enrichment Inc., Airport Road, Crowley, LA 70526
Acadian Village 800-962-9133
  200 Green Leaf Drive, Lafayette, LA 70506

CHAPTER 16

BIRDS ON
GULF BREEZES

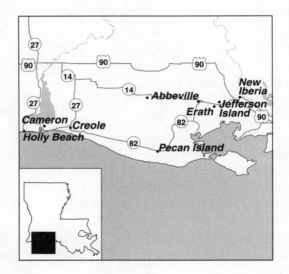

NEW IBERIA to LAKE CHARLES hugging the coast. Features gardens, shrimp boats, wetlands, beaches, birds, and gators. One hundred and sixty-five miles of straight roads and few speed zones, so tank up and take along the four b's: bird guide, binoculars, boots, and bug spray.

Outside of **New Iberia**, take Louisiana 675 southwest past U.S. Route 90 to Jefferson Island. Like its sister, Avery Island, Jefferson is not an island at all but rather a land-locked salt dome. In 1980, a hapless oil crew drilling in nearby Lake Peigneur accidentally punctured the deep underground Jefferson Island Salt Mine. A portion of the lake—including fish, boats, chunks of shore, even the badly aimed drilling rig—was sucked down like water from a bathtub. The flooded mine was abandoned, trial lawyers had a field day, and more importantly to sightseers like us, some fifty acres and several buildings of Jefferson Island's Live Oak Gardens became underwater ruins in a much deeper lake.

But the gardens have healed. Paths beneath gargantuan oaks still wind through brilliant azaleas and tulips and hibiscus and daffodils. Centerpiece is the Joseph Jefferson House, a Georgian and Steamboat Gothic retreat of the famous 1860s stage actor, now embracing art and decoy exhibits.

Where Louisiana 675 meets Louisiana 14, turn right. After crossing Bayou Peigneur into **Delcambre** (DEL-kum), take a left across the tracks to "Trawler's Row." Alongside seafood markets and ice houses berth dozens of shrimp boats, their upright masts and booms a forest. Day or night, hard-working shrimpers unload their catch, take on ice, make preparations for their next trip out. Many of the dealers (and sometimes the boats themselves) sell at retail, so this is a good place to fill up an ice chest. Each August, Delcambre becomes a festive stage for the lively pageantry of a traditional Cajun Blessing of the Fleet.

Right next door is **Erath** (EEE-rath), where fishing gives way to rice farming. On the way, watch for Smiley's dance hall. If it's Sunday evening, stop in for the old-fashioned *fais do-do*. In Erath, across the tracks on Broadway, the free Acadian Culture and Heritage Center is crammed with local artifacts. Founder Warren Perrin, a local attorney, sued the British Crown for deporting the Acadians from Nova Scotia in 1755. All he wants is an apology, but so far the Queen has remained mum. After several years, the case is still ongoing.

Louisiana 14 and the Southern Pacific tracks zip west to **Abbeville**. Take care to avoid the by-pass route in favor of Louisiana 14 Business. On the way in, the Abbey Grill, a better-than-average diner, is open twenty-four hours a day.

Blessing of the fleet

One of Louisiana's most picturesque towns, Abbeville is laid out around two squares. Filling the first is the lofty Vermilion Parish Courthouse. Go around it and a block farther to the second square where the Gothic 1911 St. Mary Magdelen Catholic Church overlooks Magdelen

Square, shady with magnificent oaks. Park, for here's a spot to stroll.

In 1843, an ambitious priest founded a frontier settlement he named Abbeville after his birthplace in France. By wresting the courthouse away from nearby Perry, he secured Abbeville's future before himself succumbing to yellow fever.

Beyond the church, the Steen's Syrup Mill flavors the air each fall. Here, for three-quarters of a century sugar cane juice has been cooked in open kettles into "sopping good" table syrup. "Nothing added, nothing extracted," the familiar yellow cans proclaim.

Later, you may want to cruise the streets behind the church and mill. Along the drowsy Vermilion River and Valmont Coulée (the word for creek in these parts), glorious Queen Anne houses bask in the shade of huge old oaks. But first, hike over to Black's Restaurant across from the church. Black's fame as a raw oyster house entices people from far and wide to drive here, but their po-boy sandwiches and other offerings are just as memorable.

In your jalopy once more, head out past the Romanesque Bank of Abbeville and the block of Italianate storefronts to the courthouse. There turn right onto Louisiana 82 south past more historic buildings. Abbeville flows into Perry; Perry into rice fields. After Louisiana 82 takes a hard right turn at Esther, distances grow long. Rice gives way to pastures which become steadily soggier heading south across the Intracoastal Waterway and through endless prairies of marsh grass. Thirty-five miles below Abbeville, a prominent treeline against the flat horizon marks **Pecan Island**.

Once again, "island" means any half-dry spot, any rise above the marsh. Pecan Island is actually a *chenière*, an ancient beach front stranded when the coast retreated seaward. Such low ridges root live oaks and pecan trees, creating the only habitable scraps along this wild coast.

Acadians arriving in Louisiana in the 1760s quickly adopted Spanish ranching methods. In less than a decade, they were driving their own herds of longhorns to New Orleans. Hardy French-speaking cowboys still run cattle in places like Pecan Island. The longhorns are gone, replaced by Black Angus, tawny white Charolais, red white-faced Herefords, and heat-and-disease resistant humped Brahmas, introduced from India in 1861.

With a bit of luck, especially on weekends, you might see a rowdy assemblage from the roadside where a *coup de main* (helping hand) is taking place. This Cajun tradition brings family, neighbors, and friends—and their gear—together to help *parquer les animaux*. Such roundups and cattle drives sometimes briefly block Louisiana 82, though nowadays when cattle take to the road it's more often in the back of a truck.

Into Cameron Parish. Of Louisiana's sixty four parishes (counties), Cameron is geographically largest yet smallest in population. Mostly wetlands, more than a quarter million acres are designated as wildlife refuge or bird sanctuary. Here, two of the greatest North American migratory bird flyways, the Central and the Mississippi, converge.

Between March and November, stop at the Rockefeller Refuge visitors center to pick up brochures. Its few wildlife exhibits are overshadowed by artifacts from *El Nuevo Constante*, an eighteenth-century Spanish wreck salvaged off the coast. A half mile farther, a graded road penetrates the eighty-four-thousand-acre coastal refuge. An observation tower, penned waterfowl and deer await—this is definitely a bug spray and boots area.

West from Rockefeller, Louisiana 82 embraces the seaward rim of **Grand Chenier**, one of the few places in coastal Louisiana where the eye discerns elevation changes. To the right, oak ridges drip Spanish moss. To the left, marsh grass flattens to a treeless horizon, the air pungent with salt. Incidentally, President Franklin Roosevelt so enjoyed a hunting trip to Grand Chenier that he thanked the parish with a new courthouse.

Shrimp boats chug gulfward as the road crosses the Mermentau River. At **Oak Grove**, Louisiana 82 takes a hard right turn. In **Creole**, it meets Louisiana 27, a short cut north to Lake Charles designated the "Creole Nature Trail."

Along the route, the U.S. Fish and Wildlife Service has a wonderful vistitors center. Exhibits will help you identify birds while a life-size animatronic Cajun woman, Tante Marie, recounts what life was like when she was a bayou child. Unlike so many acts of public-spirited wishful thinking, the name "Creole Nature Trail" fits. It really is wild and pretty.

If you don't take the turn at Oak Grove, straight ahead the parish road accesses Rutherford Beach then rejoins Louisiana 82 near the town of **Cameron**, our destination.

On June 28th, 1957, the first hurricane of the June to October season tore ashore here. Very few of the buildings you see are older than that date. Michelle's mother, back then a journalist sent to cover the catastrophe, still shows anguish as she remembers the scenes of horror. "Hundreds drowned. For days, they kept finding bodies. A lot, they never found." On the outskirts of town, at Lady of the Sea Catholic Church, rises an Italian-built shrine to the storm's victims.

To grab a bite in Cameron, try Linda Mae's or Pat's. For brochures and maps, visit the tourist bureau just east of FDR's 1938 Art Deco courthouse. A ferry runs to Monkey Island for a close-up look at a shrimp factory. From April to October, pogy (menhaden) furnish an odoriferous industry here, processing the entire fish for everything from catfood to cosmetics.

A larger twenty-four-hour ferry connects Cameron with the next span of Louisiana 82. Crossing the ship channel, jack-up barges (boats with tall legs to lift themselves out of the water) loom like skyscrapers.

Nine miles west lies **Holly Beach**, playfully dubbed the Cajun Riviera. Shops sell those wonderfully tacky souvenirs one finds at all beach resorts and nowhere else. "Camps" (summer homes built on stilts) crowd the receding shore, stepping into the waves as if on their way to Mexico. From here to Texas is naught but beaches. Shelling for conchs, cateye shells, clam-like cockles, and wine-glass-shaped whelks (Louisiana's official state shell) is best at low tide from October through March.

April and October are peak months for songbird migrations. The Holy Grail of bird watchers is to witness a "fall-out." In spring, if birds migrating over the Gulf of Mexico expanse meet storms or strong head winds, tiny wings grow very tired. Thousands of birds at a time "fall out" into the first bit of cover they spot, too exhausted to fly away even when approached. Eight miles west of Holly Beach, the Holleyman-Sheely and Henshaw Sanctuaries are especially good birding spots. Migratory butterflies, like the Monarch, also find a way station there.

From Holly Beach, turn north up Louisiana 27. This western branch of the "Creole Nature Trail" leads through the 142,000-acre Sabine National Wildlife Refuge. Established in 1937, it's the largest sanctuary on the American Gulf Coast. Right off the highway, a one-and-a-half-mile all-weather, handicap-accessible, wildlife foot trail crosses the marsh to an observation tower. A bit farther north, a visitors center offers info and interesting exhibits for the ornithologically impaired.

Bug sprayed and binoculared, we ventured onto the trail and immediately spied a roseate spoonbill, inaugurating a variety of sightings. The nearness of the path to nests caused hidden birds to shrill from the reeds in loud surprise. As the wind picked up, the constant shushing grasses hid our approach, allowing us to get close to other big pink spoonbills, dozens of herons, scores of red-winged blackbirds, and who knows how many others.

The best months for wading birds are from August to January. During warm months, you'll also spot alligators, but use common sense. Keep the family dog in the car, lest he become a snack. Don't approach them; don't throw things. Docile as they seem while sunning, they can charge if the mood strikes.

Crossing the Intracoastal Waterway bridge, marsh dries out into pasture, then farms. Louisiana 27 into **Sulphur** is a typical franchise-heavy strip, though the larger-than-life longhorn steer spinning atop Wagonwheel Barbecue and Gumbo does lend surreal charm. Sulphur's free Brimstone Museum & Welcome Center in the 1915 Southern Pacific Depot lies seven blocks west of Louisiana 27 at the end of Logan Street. The town has mined its namesake mineral since 1894 and once produced most of America's supply.

Louisiana 27 eventually bumps into U.S. Route 90 at the remains of old downtown Sulphur. Toward **Lake Charles**, U.S. Route 90 flows into Interstate 10 to pass smack dab through chemical plants and refineries before traversing the Calcasieu (KAL-ka-shoo) River. On the steep, white knuckle bridge, look for the crossed-pistol railing motifs, a homage to Jean Lafitte who once roved these waters. Nowadays, popular paddle-wheel casinos ply the city's small lake.

Take the first exit off the bridge to the Southwest Louisiana Visitors Bureau for a map to the Charpentier district of turn-of-the-century lumber-baron homes and directions to Lake Charles' many restaurants.

For more information:

Live Oak Gardens 318-365-3332
    5505 Rip Van Winkle Road, New Iberia, LA 70560
Acadian Culture & Heritage Center, Erath 318-937-6164
    Erath, LA 70533
Abbeville Tourist Bureau 318-898-4264
    1905 Veterans Memorial Drive, Abbeville, LA 70511
Rockefeller Refuge 318-538-2286
    U.S. Route 1, Box 20-B, Grand Chenier, LA 70643
Cameron Parish Tourist Commission 318-775-5493
    P.O. Box 388, Cameron, LA 70631
Holly Beach Cajun Riviera Association 318-569-2388
    HC 69, Box 74, Holly Beach, LA 70631
Holleyman-Sheely & Henshaw Sanctuaries 318-436-9588
    c/o Baton Rouge Audubon Society,
    P.O. Box 82525, Baton Rouge, LA 70884-2525
Brimstone Museum 318-527-7142
    800 Picard Road, Sulphur, LA 70663
Southwest Louisiana Visitor's Bureau 800-456-SWLA
    1211 North Lakeshore Drive, Lake Charles, LA 70601

CHAPTER 17
BORDERLANDS

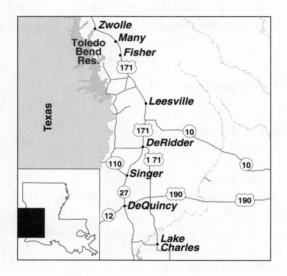

 AKE CHARLES to TOLEDO BEND along the western border of the state, through railroad and lumber towns. A hundred and twelve miles of military history, gardens, museums, fishing areas, and pine hills.

From **Lake Charles**, old U.S. Route 90 west toward Sulphur still passes under remnants of a pleasant, live-oak canopy planted by WPA workers in the 1930s. Turn north on Louisiana 27 into the honks of Sulphur's strip-mall traffic...swiftly relieved by mile after mile of idyllic pines and farms.

In the railroad town of **DeQuincy**, Louisiana 27 joins Louisiana 12 for two blocks before splitting off north again. If you stay on Louisiana 12 a bit farther, however, it angles to the DeQuincy Railroad Museum, housed in an ornate 1923 Mission Revival Kansas City Southern Depot. Leaning into ticket windows and clacking across tile floors amidst a wealth of iron-horse paraphenalia revives the days when railroad travel was not only convenient but à la mode. Outside, kids imitate conductors' calls from a restored locomotive and rail cars as mothers watch from picnic tables.

Where Louisiana 27 crosses north into Beauregard Parish, signs warning "Do Not Stop for Hitchhikers" mark Phelps Correctional Facility's sprawl into surrounding farmlands.

At **Singer**, a spur onto Louisiana 110 travels twelve miles to the 1883 Burk Log Cabin and Merryville Museum. Copious artifacts remember the area's first settlers, the Coushatta Indians who'd trudged west from Alabama to escape becoming pawns in Europeans' colonial wars, as well as more recent lumber speculators. Louisiana 110 connects with U.S. Route 190 north of Merryville to zip through pine forests into **DeRidder**.

Bypassing the Merryville detour? Stay on Louisiana 27 from Singer through rice farms, timberlands, and ranches until DeRidder, where, at the edge of town, the first USO club in the U.S. was built in 1941 to blast big-band swing into the hearts of servicemen. On the corner of Pine and Seventh Streets, the white barnlike wooden building is now, appropriately, the local Civic Center.

A right turn at the light onto U.S. Route 190 east (First Street) passes in front of DeRidder's grandly ominous Gothic jail, now undergoing restoration; and next to it, the showily elegant Beaux Arts courthouse. Imagine the awe of backwoodsmen come to town when both were completed in 1914.

A block farther, Washington Street fronts the Kansas City Southern tracks with several blocks of elaborate storefronts dating from the 1910s heyday of the longleaf-pine lumber boom. Strolling to the depot and local museum, pause to browse the Standard Lumber Commissary

building, now an antiques mall. Up the street, the handsome
Lumberman's Bank & Trust is outshone by the First National Bank.
Still open for business, its lobby and tellers' windows are marble whimsy.

At the north end of old downtown, Reichley's is run by a second
generation Rumanian baker. Locals zoom in to request, "The usual,
please," meaning yeasty German breads, sugary confections and pungent imported cheeses, sausages and hams. Mr. Boanca regaled us with
stories while unveiling more delicacies from his coolers. Loaded with
broetchen (small rolls), wurst and cheese, we headed north out of
town on U.S. Route 171 into dense second-growth pine.

Thirteen miles north of DeRidder, Louisiana 10 leaves U.S. Route
171 to cross the state west to east. A half mile past that intersection is
a gargantuan flea market. Barely restraining ourselves, we instead took
Louisiana 10 east toward **Fort Polk**.

This huge army base (three hundred and eleven square miles!)
opened in 1940 to test battlefield tactics if (and as it turned out, when)
America entered World War II. Its namesake, Leonidas Polk, whose
father and grandfather fought alongside Washington at Valley Forge,
resigned as Episcopal Bishop of Louisiana to serve as a Confederate
general during the Civil War.

Fort Polk Military Museum is tucked away in a poorly marked corner of the sprawling base. So listen up, recruits! After three miles on
Louisiana 10, go left (north) on Louisiana 467 for three-quarters of a
mile, then right on Belrichard Avenue for a half a mile. Turn left on
Mississippi and left again on South Carolina. At ease!

The packed, one-room collection of armaments, uniforms, and
other military items spans World War II to Desert Storm. Outside,
helicopters, tanks, and artillery pieces await your inspection. Hard-
core armchair warriors should ask for the self-guided base tour map.
Otherwise, Mississippi Avenue continues north, and a left on Louisiana Avenue goes through the main gates to U.S. Route 171 north.

For adventurous diners, the next several miles offer countless flavors, as the entrepreneurial spirit of German and Asian Fort Polk
dependents takes a culinary turn. Most intriguing are the cultural

amalgams, such as the Korean Kountry Kitchen in **Anacoco**.

But then, juxtapositions are the norm here. While the major local industry was training for when the Cold War got hot, it may surprise you that **New Llano** (LON-o by most, YON-o by resident old-timers) was among America's largest and most successful socialist utopian colonies. Transplanted from Los Angeles, it flourished among the pines from 1917 to 1937.

From New Llano to Leesville, U.S. Route 171 is a soldier's "liberty strip" where tattoo parlors, pawn shops, night clubs, and barnlike drive-thru liquor stores anticipate rowdy Saturday nights.

In **Leesville** proper, a right on East Fertitta Street dead ends at the 1916 Mission Revival depot now a—you guessed it—local archive. This Museum of West Louisiana celebrates "No Man's Land," the neutral territory disputed by the U.S. and Spain until 1819. Its swamps and thick woods hid renegades of many nationalities.

Just across, the stately 1915 Fertitta Brothers building still houses a hardware store and provides the start of a drive through old Leesville. Head north paralleling the tracks and an older liberty strip, to the lovely 1909 Beaux Arts courthouse in the center of a spry downtown. A left off Railroad down any number of residential streets leads back to 5th Street, which is the northbound lane of U.S. Route 171.

The Leesville area hosts many attractions. Rental canoes and expeditions explore Toro Bayou's wild natural beauty. Eighteen miles southwest on Louisiana 8, the Burr Ferry Civil War breastworks are some of the best preserved in the South. Pick-your-own blueberry farms come with the season, and rockhounds can hunt opals year round. The tourism office on U.S. Route 171 north of Leesville offers brochures and advice.

Back on U.S. Route 171 north, mountains of pine logs await the teeth of the mill under a constant mist of water to thwart bugs and prevent fires. Farther along, their still-standing brethren line up. Each copse is so uniform in age and height that "tree farm" signs are redundant.

What few towns existed here before lumbering were mostly dusty cattle-drive stopovers for Texas-beef tramping east. The 1897 arrival of the Kansas City Southern line brought the whine of sawmills and a rush of workers. Virgin timber was soon cut over, but the hills were replanted. Plywood and pulp mills arrived, too impatient for trees to reach full growth.

West from Anacoco, Louisiana 392 treks to the dam that forms the huge Toledo Bend Reservoir. Begun over much controversy by Governor Jimmie Davis in 1960 and completed in 1969, this cooperative venture between Texas and Louisiana stretches north for seventy renowned-for-fishing miles. Campgrounds, motels, and marinas dot the length of the lake, but we decided to save our visit for farther up the road.

Seventeen miles north of Leesville, still on U.S. Route 171, a large motel dwarfs the entrance to Hodges Gardens. Back in the early days of motor touring, this was one of the South's premier attractions. It still is. Promoted as the world's largest private arboretum, Hodges represents an early-twentieth-century industrialist's transformation of an abandoned quarry and surrounding cut-over woodland into a showpiece of reforestation.

Inviting gardens, lovely year round, become spectacular with March tulips and April azaleas. As a kid, Michelle and her cousins bounded these stepped walkways and twisting paths while her mother and aunts fantasized about replanting their gardens back home to match this exquisite color.

While exploring these knolls, keep eyes alert for red-cockaded woodpeckers, an endangered species occasionally spotted in the area. Look among live pines for the bird's horizontally striped "ladder back" markings and listen for its loud, nasal "yank, yank." Don't be fooled though, for its cockade of red feathers is so tiny it's virtually invisible. If you encounter a ladder-backed woodpecker with a noticeably red head... Sorry, it's probably the larger, more common red-bellied variety.

North of Hodges Gardens, pine trees push U.S. Route 171 into a narrower channel. Hills rise more steeply, like a whip of ribbon. At the turnoff to historic **Fisher**, hit the brakes. Pull off the road. Look for a rusty pick-up truck and hitched to it a red plywood trailer emblazoned, "You can eat Edmonson's beef with no teeth. Try It!"

We're serious. Edmonson's barbecue is exquisite, with or without your teeth. Buy it by the pound or in sandwiches. Mr. Edmonson also sells tasty Zwolle tamales, but "Brisket is the crowd pleaser," he freely announces. "And the sauce is the boss." He's right. Savoring each sloppy bite, we headed left on Fisher Road (Main Street) toward the village center.

Built in 1899 by the Louisiana Long Leaf Lumber Company, Fisher's store, opera house, office building, and silk-stocking row of managers' homes form an unspoiled company town. Sold to Boise Cascade in 1966, the historical society has proudly taken over the upkeep. A modern sawmill still operates behind the town, but the old train station now contains the public library and police station, and little theater productions have replaced traveling variety shows and silent pictures at the majestic opera house.

Inside the cavernous store, a fleamarket spreads over the endless hardwood floors and shelves with rolling stepladders. It doesn't take much to conjure up the days when workers paid in script were a captive market here for everything from cribs to coffins. Fisher's Sawmill Days in May re-create that era.

Five miles north is **Many** (MAN-ee), another busy crossroads/courthouse/timber town. The Mission Revival Catholic Church is a centerpiece; one wonders if its architecture is drawn from the area's Spanish influence or from the prevailing style of Kansas City Southern depots. Heading northeast on Louisiana 6, turn south onto Louisiana 3118 to Geoghagan Road and Fort Jesup Commemorative Area.

As we arrived, manager Donna Spears was repairing the hem of her period costume, it having caught fire during a demonstration of 1830s cooking methods. Though this out-of-the-way site is quiet now, Ms. Spears told how, "back in 1845 literally half the American army was stationed here, marshaled to invade Mexico." Dragoons (elite troops with fancy bucketlike helmets), horse soldiers (unlike true cavalry, they dismounted to fight), and other top-echelon warriors occupied the post.

On the highest hill around, its true strategic importance was its location near the border of the nine-year-old Republic of Texas.

Fort Jesup's hotel, theater, school, gymnasium, and soldier-tended garden plots made it a coveted assignment. Social events were numerous, from regimental band concerts to raucous gander-pulling (ask your guide if you dare). Of the original eighty-two structures, only the kitchen remains. Reconstructed officers quarters house the interpretive museum.

Backtrack on Louisiana 6 through Many and west to Toledo Bend Reservoir past roadside emporiums and factory-direct fishing-tackle outlets. On a finger of land where Louisiana 6 goes over a causeway to Texas, the Sabine River Authority Welcome Center is perfect for gathering info on fishing and camping and for strolling around its picnic grounds where lanky pines overlook the sparkling lake.

Named by a homesick Spanish explorer, Toledo Bend's primitive campsites are tucked in its wild, unspoiled terrain. Popular rental cabins peep from the shores. (Advance reservations are very much advised.)

From the lake, backtrack to Louisiana 191. A short hop north is Louisiana Treasures, a factory outlet and showroom for scrumptious jellies and sauces made from local fruits, especially the red mayhaw, a Southern culinary treasure. Mayhaw's flavor is mild, a bit like plum jelly, but of course much better.

Louisiana 191 continues north over fingers of Toledo Bend to **Zwolle** (ZWA-lee). Despite its Dutch name, Zwolle is closer in culture to the American Southwest. Many residents trace their ancestry to Apache Indians brought here as slaves in Spanish colonial days.

Foodways reflect that heritage during the Zwolle Tamale Fiesta, an early-October blow-out when locals claim the town "grows ten times over." No matter the month, virtually every quick stop sells the spicy tamales. For a sit-down meal, try Bill & Sissy's, east of town on U.S. Route 171 south, where a mural depicts a crying pig dreaming of hot sauce and onions.

From Zwolle, U.S. Route 171 leads north to **Mansfield** (the end of Chapter 2.) Or head back to Many, then east along old El Camino Real (Louisiana 6) to Natchitoches's many historic treasures.

But we took a short drive west on Louisiana 191 to Louisiana 3229 and North Toledo Bend State Park. With cabins, campsites, and a visitors center, it's arguably the prettiest spot on all Toledo Bend. Arm in arm, we listened to the rustle of the pines and watched the sunset dance on the glistening ripples of the lake, reveling once more in Louisiana's unending marvels.

For more information:

DeQuincy Railroad Museum 318-786-7113
    P.O. Box 997, DeQuincy, LA 70633
Merryville Museum 318-825-6372
    Highway 90, Merryville, LA 70653
Beauregard Parish/DeRidder Tourist Commission 318-463-5534
    624 High School Drive, DeRidder, LA 70634
Fort Polk Military Museum 318-531-7905
    Buildings 916 & 917,
    South Carolina Avenue, Fort Polk, LA 71459
Museum of West Louisiana 318-239-0927
    803 South Third Street, Leesville, LA 71446
Vernon Parish/Leesville Tourist Commission 318-238-0783
    P.O. Box 1228, Leesville, LA 71496-1228
Hodges Gardens 318-586-3523
    P.O. Box 900, Many, LA 71449
Fort Jesup State Commemorative Area 318-256-4117
    Route 2, Box 611, Many, LA 71449
Sabine River Authority (Toledo Bend) 800-259-LAKE
    15091 Texas Highway, Many, LA 71449
North Toledo Bend State Park 318-645-4715
    P.O. Box 56, Zwolle, LA 71486

INDEX

Titles in the Country Roads series:

Country Roads of Alabama $10.95
Country Roads of Connecticut and Rhode Island
Country Roads of Florida
Country Roads of Georgia
Country Roads of Hawaii
Country Roads of Idaho
Country Roads of Illinois, second edition
Country Roads of Indiana
Country Roads of Iowa
Country Roads of Kentucky
Country Roads of Louisiana $10.95
Country Roads of Maine
Country Roads of Maritimes
Country Roads of Maryland and Delaware
Country Roads of Massachusetts
Country Roads of Michigan, second edition
Country Roads of Minnesota
Country Roads of Missouri
Country Roads of New Hampshire, second edition
Country Roads of New Jersey, second edition $10.95
Country Roads of New York
Country Days in New York City
Country Roads of North Carolina
Country Roads of Ohio, second edition $10.95
Country Roads of Ontario
Country Roads of Oregon
Country Roads of Pennsylvania
Country Roads of Southern California
Country Roads of Tennessee
Country Roads of Texas
Country Roads of Vermont
Country Roads of Virginia
Country Roads of Washington
Country Roads of Wisconsin $10.95

All other prices, $9.95. All books are available at bookstores. Prices subject to change.
Or order directly from the publisher (add $3.00 shipping & handling for direct orders):

Country Roads Press
P.O. Box 838
Oaks, Pennsylvania 19456
(610) 666-9763

Country Roads Press

Country Roads Press publishes books that celebrate the spirit and flavor of rural and small town America. Far from strip malls and chain stores, the heart of America may still be found among the people and in the places along its country roads. Country Roads Press invites its readers to travel those roads with us.